I0529973

THE ESSENTIAL GIRL'S GUIDE TO PUBERTY & PERIODS

UNDERSTAND YOUR BODY, EMBRACE THE CHANGES & GROW-UP WITH EMOTIONAL AND PHYSICAL CONFIDENCE

DEBBIEANN LEWIS

© Copyright DebbieAnn Lewis 2025 - All rights reserved.

The Essential Girl's Guide To Puberty & Periods; Understand Your Body, Embrace the Changes & Grow-up with Emotional and Physical Confidence

The content within this book may not be reproduced, duplicated or transmitted without direct written permission from the author or the publisher.

Under no circumstances will any blame or legal responsibility be held against the publisher, or author, for any damages, reparation, or monetary loss due to the information contained within this book. Either directly or indirectly. You are responsible for your own choices, actions, and results.

Legal Notice:

This book is copyright protected. This book is only for personal use. You cannot amend, distribute, sell, use, quote or paraphrase any part, of the content within this book, without the consent of the author or publisher.

Disclaimer Notice:

Please note the information contained within this document is for educational and entertainment purposes only. All effort has been expended to present accurate, up-to-date, and reliable, complete information. No warranties of any kind are declared or implied. Readers acknowledge that the author is not engaging in the rendering of legal, financial, medical or professional advice. The content within this book has been derived from various sources. Please consult a licensed professional before attempting any techniques outlined in this book.

By reading this document, the reader agrees that under no circumstances is the author responsible for any losses, direct or indirect, which are incurred as a result of the use of the information contained within this document, including, but not limited to, — errors, omissions, or inaccuracies.

CONTENTS

INTRODUCTION

There was a time when I sat with my niece, Ella, at the kitchen table. She had that look. You know, the one that says, "I have a question, but I don't know how to ask it." We were making cookies, and I could tell something was on her mind. Finally, she blurted out, "Auntie, what's a period?" Her cheeks turned pink, and I could see she felt awkward. But that's the thing about growing up—it's full of questions and changes that can feel a little strange at first.

This book is for every girl who has ever felt like Ella. It is here to be a supportive guide as you go through puberty and start your period. Think of it as a friendly companion to help you through this important time. With this book, you'll have a trusted friend to turn to whenever you have questions or need a little reassurance.

My vision for this book is simple. I want it to be a resource that helps you understand and embrace the changes happening in your body, from a girl to a woman and someday even a mother. It blends facts with emotional support, giving you the knowledge and confidence you need. Puberty can feel overwhelming, but with the right information, you can face it with courage and confidence.

This book is for you if you're between the ages of 8 and 14. It's written with you in mind, knowing what you are going through and what you're curious about. We'll talk about everything from body changes to feelings, making sure you feel prepared for each new step.

What makes this book special is the personal stories and interactive parts. You'll find real-life stories from girls just like you and activities to help you discover more about yourself. These features make it more than just a book—it's an experience that is both fun and informative.

Let me tell you a little about myself. I'm a daughter, sister, mom, aunt, friend, and grandmother. I've been there with my own daughter and granddaughters and nieces, guiding them through these years. I also worked as a nurse's aide, girl's camp counselor, and mentor, giving me valuable experience in helping them understand their health and their bodies. I've written this book to share what I've learned and to help you feel supported.

Throughout the book, we'll explore key themes like self-care and body positivity. You'll learn how to take care of yourself and appreciate your body. We'll talk about emotional strength, helping you build resilience as you grow. We'll also celebrate diversity, recognizing that everyone's journey is unique and special in its own way.

I encourage you to engage with this book. Use it as a tool for learning about yourself. Reflect on what you read, and take part in the activities. This book is here to empower you, and the more you engage with it, the more you'll gain from it.

As you turn the pages, remember that this book is committed to being your reliable guide. It's here to support you every step of the way. Let's dive in together and make this journey through puberty a positive and empowering experience. You're not alone, and I'm here with you.

1

UNDERSTANDING YOUR
CHANGING BODY

I remember a time when I visited my daughter's school for a parent-teacher meeting. I sat on one of those small chairs, looking at the tiny desks. Then, I noticed the kids playing outside. Some of them were the same height as the teachers! It was like watching a field of sunflowers where some sprout up overnight, reaching towards the sky, while others take their time. It reminded me of how growing up can be so unpredictable and fast. One moment, you're fitting into your favorite jeans, and the next, you're wondering if you've entered a magical land where your shoes have shrunk overnight. This is what we call a growth spurt, and it's a big part of puberty. So, let's talk about what's happening with your body because it's pretty amazing. You're not just growing taller; you're growing up in every way.

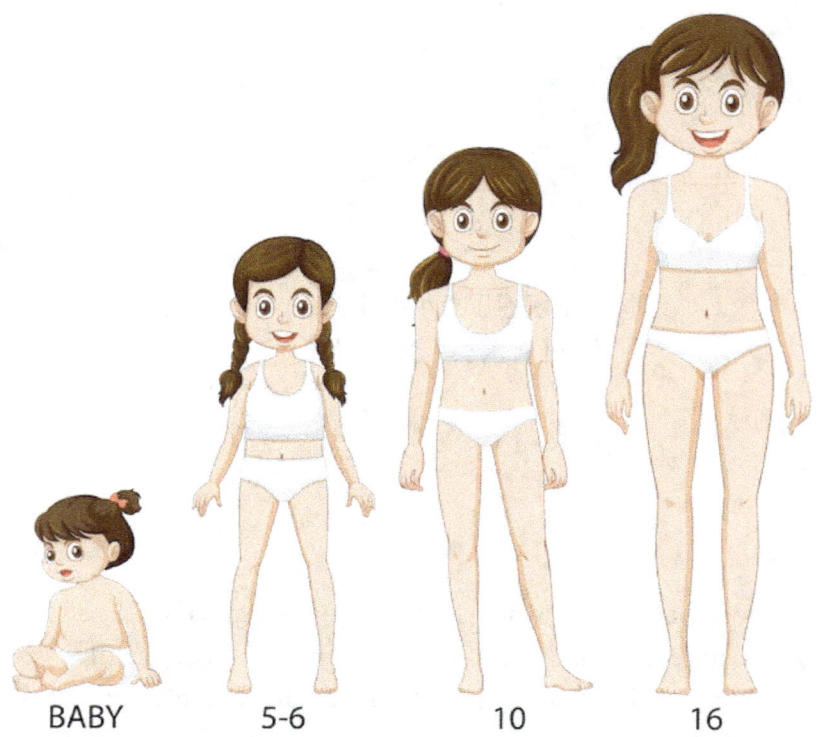

BABY   5-6   10   16

1.1 THE MYSTERY OF GROWTH SPURTS

Have you ever woken up and felt like you grew an inch overnight? It's like your bones have decided to stretch while you sleep. This is called a growth spurt. It's a regular part of puberty. During this time, your body produces more of a special hormone called the growth hormone. This hormone tells your body it's time to grow, and it gets to work when you're resting. Sleep is super important during this time. It's like your body's secret workshop, where all the magic happens. So when your parents remind you to get to bed early, it's not just to annoy you. It's because your body needs that rest to grow strong and healthy.

As your body grows, you might notice your pants feel shorter and your sleeves don't quite reach your wrists anymore. Your feet might outgrow your shoes faster than you'd like. This is because your body is making room for all the new changes. You might find yourself bumping into things or feeling a bit clumsy. That's okay. It's normal. Your body is getting used to its new size, and soon, you'll have it all figured out. It's like learning to ride a bike all over again.

You might worry because your friends are growing at different rates. Some might shoot up like a beanstalk, while others grow slowly. Everyone's body has its own timeline. It's okay to be different. Your height and size will change when your body is ready. Comparing yourself to others is like comparing apples to oranges. Everyone is unique, and your body knows what it's doing. Everybody grows according to their own DNA.

While all these changes happen, it's important to keep your body healthy and active. Eating a balanced diet helps your body grow strong. Foods rich in calcium and protein, like milk, cheese, and beans, are great for your bones and muscles. It's also important to move your body. Fun activities like dancing, swimming, or playing sports help keep you fit and strong. You don't have to be perfect at them. Just have fun and enjoy moving your body.

Reflection Section: How Tall Will You Be?

- Grab a piece of paper and write down your parents' heights.
- Use this simple formula: Add their heights together. For girls, subtract five inches and divide by two. For boys, add five inches and divide by two. This can give you a rough idea of your future height.

- Remember, it's just for fun and not set in stone. Your body will grow at its own pace.

Growing up can feel like a whirlwind at times. One day you're running around, and the next, you're towering over your friends. But each part of this change is special. Your body knows what it needs to do, and it's doing it just as it's meant to do. So take care of it, be patient, and enjoy the ride. You're on your way to becoming the wonderful person you're meant to be.

1.2 YOUR BODY'S BLUEPRINT: UNDERSTANDING BREAST DEVELOPMENT

Breast development can feel like a big deal, especially when it starts to happen unexpectedly. You might notice small bumps or breast buds under your nipples, which can be a little tender. This is the beginning of what doctors call Tanner Stage 1. It's the first sign that your body is getting ready for the changes of puberty. As you move into Tanner Stage 2, those bumps start to grow, and you'll notice your breasts getting a bit fuller. This is when you begin to see the changes happening more clearly. By Tanner Stage 3, your breasts may start to take on a more rounded shape. Tanner Stage 4 follows, where the areola and nipple form a secondary mound on top of the breast tissue. Finally, Tanner Stage 5 is when you reach a mature breast shape, though this can continue to change as you grow. Every woman goes through these stages differently. Some girls may start early, while others might not notice changes until later. And that's perfectly fine.

Uneven development is common. You might see one breast growing faster than the other. This can feel strange, but it's normal. Your body is just taking its time to even things out. Many girls experience tenderness or soreness as their breasts grow. This can make things like hugging or wearing tight tops a bit uncomfortable. But remember, these feelings are temporary. Your body is simply adjusting to its new changes. It's similar to how your muscles feel sore after trying a new sport. It's a sign that things are happening, and soon, it will all feel normal again.

Buying your first bra can be a fun and empowering experience. But it can also feel a bit daunting with so many options out there. For starters, a simple training bra is a good choice. It offers light support and coverage without any wires. As you grow, you might want something with more support. Soft-cup bras or sports bras are comfortable choices that can provide the support you need. The right fit is important. A well-fitted bra can make you feel more comfortable and confident. When trying on bras, make sure the band sits snugly around your body, and the straps don't dig into your shoulders. You should feel supported but not restricted.

Body image can feel challenging, especially when you see images in magazines or on social media. These pictures often show people who look perfect. But remember, everyone is unique, and real life is full of diversity. Models and celebrities often have teams of people to help them look a certain way. That's not real life. Every body is different, and that's what makes us all special. It's important to practice self-affirmation. Remind yourself of your strengths and what you love about yourself. Stand in front of the mirror and say, "I like my smile" or "I am strong." It might feel silly at first, but words have power. They can help you build a positive image of yourself.

Reflection Section: My Body, My Rules

- Spend a few moments each day in front of the mirror.
- Choose one thing you like about yourself and say it out loud. It can be anything, like your hair, your kindness, or your ability to make others laugh.
- Write it down in a journal. Over time, notice how your list grows.

Remember, your body is your own. It's okay to feel unsure or awkward sometimes. These changes are a natural part of growing up. Every stage is a step towards becoming who you are meant to be: an amazing young woman, beautiful and complete. Embrace the uniqueness of your journey, and be kind to yourself along the way.

1.3 NAVIGATING THE HAIRY TRUTH: HAIR GROWTH EXPLAINED

One day, you might notice tiny hairs sprouting in places where there was none before. It can feel a bit like discovering a surprise garden growing on your body. This happens under your arms, thicker hair on your calves and also around your pubic area, around and between your legs. It is a normal part of puberty. This hair growth is one of the signs that your body is changing, and it's all thanks to hormones. Hormones are like little messengers that tell your body what to do. During puberty, they signal your body to start growing hair in these new places. It might feel strange at first, but soon it will become just another part of your daily life.

When it comes to grooming all this new hair, you have choices. Some girls decide to shave, others might try waxing, and some might leave it natural. It's all about what feels right for you. Shaving is quick and easy, but it requires regular upkeep. Waxing lasts longer, but it can be a bit painful, as well as expensive to keep up. Choosing to keep your body hair natural is perfectly fine, too. It's important to know that there is no right or wrong way. What matters is what makes you feel comfortable and confident. Remember, different cultures have different views on body hair. In some places, keeping hair natural is celebrated, while in others, removing it is common. It's all about personal choice and what feels best for you.

There are lots of myths about body hair that you might hear from friends or online. One common myth is that shaving makes hair grow back thicker or faster. This isn't true. Hair might feel different as it grows back, but it's the same as before. It can feel tempting to do what everyone else is doing, especially if you see your friends making certain choices. But remember, it's your body, and you get to decide what's best for you. It's okay to be different. Making informed choices is empowering. You can decide what makes you feel good and what fits with your lifestyle.

Keeping clean is important, especially as these changes happen. Regular washing, bathing and showering helps you feel fresh and clean. Make sure to wash under your arms and around your pubic area with mild soap and water. This helps remove sweat and oils that can build up. Using deodorant can help too, especially if you notice a change in body odor. That odor can resemble a raw onion smell or a dirty clothes smell, which most people find offensive. Deodorant works by reducing the bacteria that causes odors, keeping you fresh throughout the day. Choose one that feels good on your skin. There are many options, so try a few until you find one you like.

Exercise: My Hair, My Choice

- Take a few minutes and think about what you want when it comes to body hair.
- Write down how you feel about shaving, waxing, or keeping it natural. This is just for you, so be honest.
- Remember, your choice might change over time, and that's okay too.

Puberty can feel like a whirlwind of changes. Hair growth is just one part of it. It's a sign that your body is doing what it's supposed to do, maturing into an adult woman. Embrace these changes as they come. They are part of what makes you unique and special.

1.4 SKIN DEEP: ACNE AND SKIN CHANGES DURING PUBERTY

You wake up one morning, look in the mirror, and there it is—a red bump right on your forehead. Acne can feel like it appears out of nowhere. But there's a reason behind these pesky blemishes or zits. During puberty, your body goes through many changes. Hormones play a big role in this. They cause your skin to produce more oil, called sebum. This oil can mix with dead skin cells and block your pores. When pores get blocked, it creates a perfect spot for bacteria to grow, leading to those familiar red bumps. Diet and stress can also affect your skin. Eating lots of greasy foods or feeling stressed out can sometimes make acne worse. Keeping a balanced diet and finding ways to relax can help keep your skin healthier.

Taking care of your skin doesn't have to be complicated. You don't need shelves full of fancy products. Start with a gentle cleansing routine. Wash your face twice a day with a mild cleanser. Avoid scrubbing too hard, as this can irritate your skin. Remember to hydrate by drinking plenty of water. Water helps your skin stay soft and clear. Sun protection is also key. Use sunscreen daily, even on cloudy days. The sun can cause skin damage and make acne scars more noticeable. Keeping things simple but consistent can make a big difference in how your skin looks and feels.

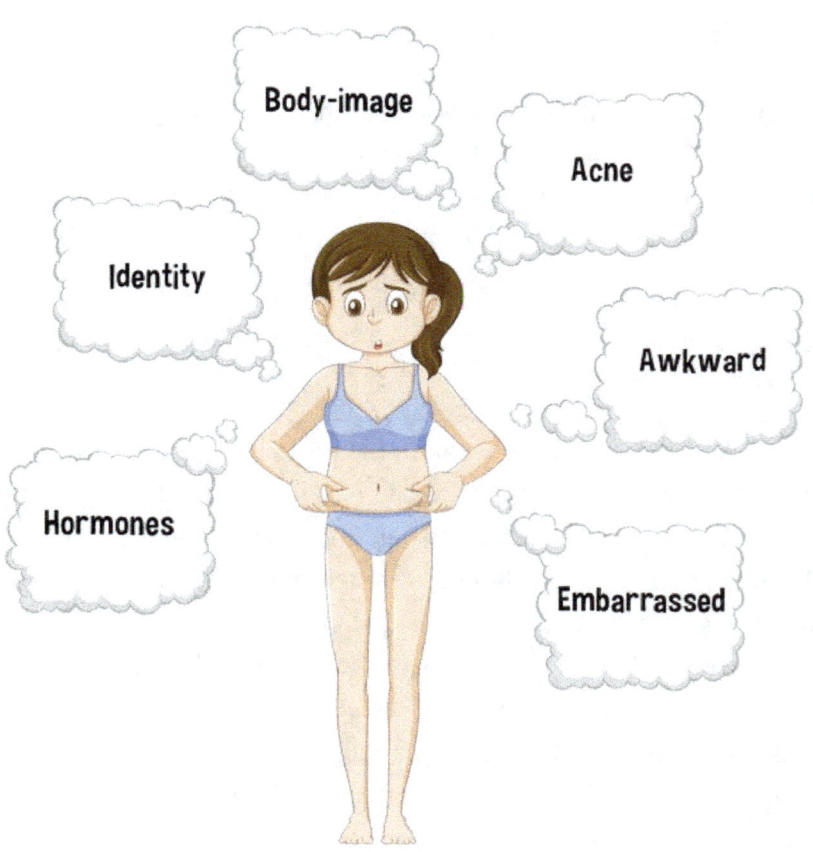

Acne can be tough on self-esteem. When you see a new pimple, you might feel like everyone is staring at it. But remember, everyone gets blemishes. Even adults get them. It's a normal part of life. Instead of focusing on the negative, practice positive self-talk. Look in the mirror and say to yourself, "I am more than my skin." It helps to remember that what's inside counts more. Self-care is also important. Take time for activities that make you feel good. Maybe it's reading a book or taking a walk. Doing things you love can help you feel more confident and happy.

You might hear a lot of myths about acne. Some people say using harsh products will clear it up quickly. But that's not true. Overusing strong products can irritate your skin and make things worse. Acne won't disappear overnight. It takes time and care. Stick to a gentle routine and be patient. Consistency is key. Some treatments promise instant results, but they often don't deliver. It's better to take a steady approach and give your skin the time it needs to heal.

Remember, your skin tells the story of your body growing and changing. It's part of your unique journey through puberty.

1.5 THE INSIDE STORY: INTERNAL CHANGES IN YOUR BODY

Your body is like a busy orchestra, and during puberty, it tunes up for a grand performance. At the heart of this transformation are your ovaries. These small, almond-shaped organs sit inside your pelvis. They act as both a factory and a storage unit. They produce hormones like estrogen and release eggs. Each month, one of these eggs takes a journey through your fallopian tubes to your uterus. It's a fascinating process that happens without you even thinking about it. Your uterus, which might seem like a mystery now, plays a big role, in being a woman and a mother. It's a pear-shaped organ that changes during your menstrual cycle. The lining thickens to prepare for a potential pregnancy. If no pregnancy happens, this lining sheds, and that's what causes your period.

Understanding these changes helps you see how your body is preparing for the future. The start of your period marks the beginning of your menstrual cycle. It's a sign that your body is becoming fertile, meaning it can support a pregnancy someday. But don't worry, getting your period is just one part of growing up. It doesn't mean you're ready for anything beyond that. It's just your body's way of showing it's healthy and doing what it's supposed to do. Reproductive health is about more than just periods. It's about recognizing how your body works and taking care of it, so it stays healthy and strong.

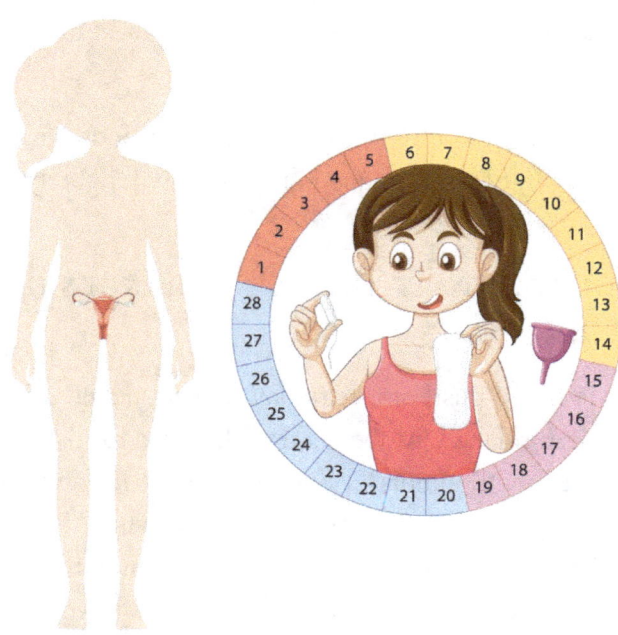

With this comes a lot of questions and sometimes worries. You might wonder about period pain or cramps. Many girls feel cramps during their periods. It's caused by your uterus contracting to help shed its lining. It might feel like a dull ache in your lower belly or back. Some girls also feel tired or moody, which is totally normal. Everyone's cycle is different. Some girls have regular periods that come like clockwork. Others might have irregular cycles. They might skip a month or have longer cycles. Your body is unique, and so is your cycle. If you have concerns about pain or irregularities, talking to a trusted adult or doctor can help.

Taking care of yourself during this time is important. Pay attention to your body. Recognize symptoms that might need attention. Severe pain, heavy bleeding, or periods that stop for a long time are worth checking with a doctor. Don't shy away from seeking medical advice. It's a smart move and helps keep you healthy. Regular check-ups can also provide reassurance. They can help answer any questions you might have about your body. Practicing good hygiene is also key. Change pads or tampons regularly to stay fresh and avoid infection. Maintain a balanced diet and stay active. These habits help your body function at its best.

Your body is doing amazing things. It's working hard to grow and change, preparing for the life ahead. There's a lot to learn, and it might seem overwhelming. Just remember, it's all part of growing up. You have the power to understand and care for your body. Listen to it, learn about it, and treat it with kindness.

1.6 HORMONES UNMASKED: THE ROLE THEY PLAY IN PUBERTY

Have you ever wondered what makes all these changes happen in your body during puberty? It's like a team of tiny messengers called hormones at work behind the scenes. These hormones are like little guides that tell your body when it's time to start changing. Two of the main hormones, estrogen and progesterone, play a huge role in this process. They signal your body to start developing in new ways. Estrogen helps with the growth of your reproductive organs and other physical changes, while progesterone supports those changes. Together, they are responsible for many of the changes you experience. You might notice changes in your mood or sudden growth in certain areas like weight gain, growing taller, breast development, etc. of your body. These are all signs that your hormones are doing their job.

The timeline of these hormonal changes can vary from person to person. Some girls might start experiencing changes as early as eight years old, while others might not notice anything until their teen years. The start of puberty marks the beginning of this hormonal activity. It's like your body has been given the green light to start developing. Over time, these hormones will continue to guide your body's growth and prepare it for adulthood. You'll notice that your body goes through cycles, especially as you begin menstruating. These cycles are a result of the hormonal fluctuations that are natural and necessary.

As hormones do their work, you might find yourself on an emotional roller coaster. One minute you're happy, and the next, you might feel sad or upset for no reason. This is completely normal. Hormonal changes can affect your mood and emotions. It's important to know that these feelings are okay. Everyone experiences mood swings during puberty. You're not alone in this. Finding ways to manage these emotions can help. Try deep breathing, journaling, or talking to someone you trust. These techniques can help you feel more in control and balanced.

Talking about what you're going through can make a big difference. Sometimes, just sharing your feelings with someone can help you feel better. Whether it's a parent, guardian, or another trusted adult, they can offer support and reassurance. They've all been through similar changes and can understand what you're experiencing. Don't hesitate to reach out. If you have questions about your hormones or the changes you're experiencing, talking to a healthcare professional can also help. They can provide information and guidance to help you understand what's happening with your body.

As you grow, remember that these hormonal changes are just a part of growing up. They are a sign that your body is developing and preparing for adulthood. Embrace these changes, and know that they are leading you into a new and exciting chapter of your life. You're not alone in this. Every woman has walked this path before you, and there's a whole community of support ready to help you along the way. Embrace your body for all it does and all it will do. You're becoming who you are meant to be, and that's something truly special.

2

EMBRACING MENSTRUATION

I magine you're at a sleepover with your best friends. You're all in your pajamas, giggling about who has a crush on whom, and trying out new hairstyles. Suddenly, one of your friends whispers that she's just started her period, and she's not sure what to do. You all gather around, offering support, advice, and even a spare pad. It's moments like these that show how important it is to understand what's happening in your body. Menstruation might seem mysterious at first, but it's just another part of growing up. Let's explore what really happens during your menstrual cycle and why it's nothing to be worried about.

Your menstrual cycle is like a monthly story your body tells. It has four main phases, each with its own chapter. It starts with the menstrual phase. This is when your period begins. It usually lasts from three to seven days. During this time, your body sheds the lining of the uterus because there's no pregnancy. This shedding is what causes the bleeding you see. It's a sign that your body is healthy and working as it should. Next comes the follicular phase.

This phase overlaps with menstruation and continues until about day thirteen. During this time, your body is busy preparing a new egg in your ovaries. Estrogen levels rise, helping to thicken the uterus lining again. This creates a cozy home ready for a potential new life.

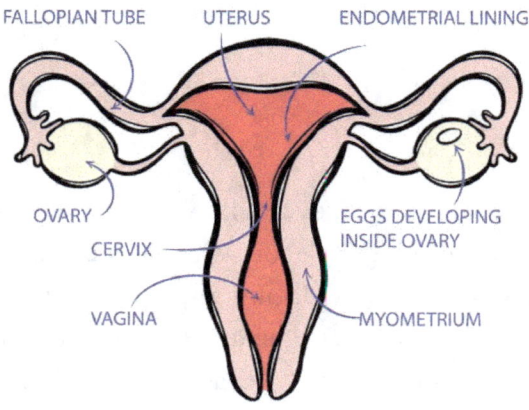

FEMALE
REPRODUCTIVE SYSTEM

Around day fourteen, the ovulation phase kicks in. This is when the mature egg is released from the ovary. It's a bit like a race, with the egg making its way through the fallopian tube. This phase is short, lasting only about twenty-four hours. But it's an important part of the cycle. If the egg meets sperm during this time, pregnancy can happen. If not, the cycle continues. The final phase is the luteal phase, from day fifteen to the next period. The empty follicle turns into the corpus luteum, which releases progesterone. This hormone further prepares the uterus lining. If pregnancy doesn't occur, hormone levels drop, and the cycle starts over with menstruation.Then the shedding begins again, you see the period blood for 3-7 days, which is when you'll need pads or your preferred method to absorb the menstrual flow.

Not everyone has the same cycle length. While a typical cycle lasts about twenty-eight days, it can vary. Your cycle might be a little shorter or longer, and that's perfectly normal. Factors like stress, diet, and even changes in routine can affect your cycle. Remember, just like many things in life, there's no perfect cycle, only what's normal for you. It's important to know that variations are natural. Some months might be slightly off, and that's okay. Your body is not a machine. It's a living, changing system that adapts to different situations.

Hormones play a big role in how your cycle works. During the follicular phase, estrogen levels rise, helping your body prepare for ovulation. This hormone can make you feel more energetic and social. When ovulation happens, there's a spike in luteinizing hormone (LH), which releases the egg. After ovulation, the luteal phase begins, and progesterone levels increase. This hormone can make you feel calmer but might also cause PMS (pre-menstrual-syndrome) symptoms like food cravings or mood swings. It's like your body has its own rhythm, guided by these hormones. Understanding this can help you make sense of how you feel throughout the month.

Tracking your cycle can be a helpful tool. It's like keeping a calendar of your body's schedule. You can use a physical calendar or a period tracking app on your phone, tablet or computer. These tools help you predict when your period will start. They also let you track symptoms like cramps or mood changes. Knowing your pattern can give you a sense of control. It helps you plan ahead, like carrying supplies when you know your period is due. Apps like

Clue or Flo offer easy ways to keep track. They provide insights into your cycle and help you learn more about your body.

Reflection Section: Track Your Cycle

- Start by marking the first day of your period on a calendar or in your app.
- Note any symptoms you experience, like cramps or headaches.
- After a few months, see if you notice any patterns.
- Use this information to prepare for future cycles, like packing supplies in advance.

Understanding your menstrual cycle helps you see it as a normal part of life. It's a sign of health and growth. By learning about each phase and what it means, you can feel more confident and in tune with your body. You're not alone in this; every girl all around the world will go through these shared experiences. Embrace this knowledge and use it to empower yourself.

2.1 FIRST PERIOD PREP: WHAT TO EXPECT AND HOW TO PREPARE

Picture this: you're going about your day, maybe feeling a bit off. You're unsure why, but something just feels different. This could be your body's way of giving you a heads-up that your first period is on its way. Some girls notice signs a few days before it happens. You might feel slight cramps in your lower belly or have mood swings. Your breasts might feel tender, or you may notice a bit of bloating. These are all normal signs that your body is preparing for menstruation. It's helpful to know these signs so you're not caught off guard. Having a period emergency kit ready can make all the difference. In a small pouch, pack a couple of pads or tampons, some tissues, and a clean pair of underwear. You might want to add some wet wipes and a little hand sanitizer. Keep this kit in your backpack or locker, just in case.

Emotions can run high when you think about your first period. It's a mix of excitement and nervousness. You might wonder if you'll be ready. The truth is, there's no way to predict the exact moment it will happen, but you can still be prepared. Remember, getting your first period is a normal part of growing up. It's a sign that your body is functioning as it should. Talking about it can help ease some of the anxiety. Find someone you trust, like a parent, guardian, or school nurse, and share your thoughts. They can offer guidance and reassurance. It's comforting to know someone has your back and understands what you're going through.

There are a lot of myths surrounding the first period, and they can cause unnecessary fear. One common worry is the fear of leaks. This can happen, especially if your flow is heavy or unexpected. Wearing a pad or period underwear can help prevent leaks. It's also a good idea to check your supplies throughout the day. Changing your pad or tampon regularly will keep you feeling fresh and secure. Another myth is that your first period will be very painful or heavy. In reality, it varies for everyone. Some girls experience little discomfort, while others might have mild cramps. Knowing these facts can help calm your fears.

Different cultures have unique ways of marking this milestone. In some cultures, the first period is celebrated with rituals or special ceremonies. It's a way to honor this change and welcome you into a new phase of life. These traditions can vary widely. Some might involve a family gathering or a small gift to mark the occasion. Others might include a special meal or symbolic gesture. These practices remind us that menstruation is a natural and respected part of life. Learning about these diverse perspectives can be fascinating and inspiring. It shows that while we all experience it differently, there's a shared understanding of its significance of life and woman-hood in being able to bear a child and become a mother.

Whether your first period comes as a surprise or you sense it approaching, being prepared can make it feel less daunting. It's a new chapter that brings with it a blend of emotions and experiences. Embrace it with confidence and curiosity, knowing you're not alone. There's a world of knowledge and support waiting for you.

2.2 PERIOD PRODUCTS 101: CHOOSING WHAT'S RIGHT FOR YOU

Selecting the right period products can feel as overwhelming as picking a treat in a candy store—there are so many choices! Let's break it down to make things easier.

Pads and Panty Liners

Pads are often the first choice for beginners because they're familiar and easy to use. They stick to the inside of your underwear and catch the period blood as it leaves your body. Pads and panty liners come in various sizes and absorbencies, from ultra-thin to overnight, making them versatile for different needs. They're comfortable and simple to use, but some may find them bulky, especially during physical activities.

Pads need to be changed every 1–4 hours. To dispose of a pad, peel it off your underwear, fold it in half with the sticky side out, and wrap it in tissue paper, the wrapper it came in, or a small disposal bag. Toss it in the trash—never flush a pad down the toilet, as it can clog plumbing.

Tampons

Tampons are small and fit inside your body to absorb period blood, making them ideal for activities like swimming or sports. Inserting a tampon might feel tricky at first, but it gets easier with practice. Start with the smallest size, relax, and follow the package instructions.

Change tampons every 4–8 hours. When removing one, wrap it in toilet paper or a disposal bag and throw it in the trash. Avoid flushing tampons, even though they seem small—they can cause plumbing issues.

Menstrual Cups

Menstrual cups are small, flexible cups made of medical-grade silicone. They're inserted into the vagina to collect period blood and can stay in place for up to 12 hours, making them convenient for busy days. To remove the cup, pinch the base to release the seal before pulling it out. Rinse the cup with water and reinsert. Cups are reusable and environmentally friendly, but they do require comfort with your body and a little practice to use effectively.

Period Underwear

Period underwear looks like regular panties but has special layers to absorb period blood. Depending on the brand, they can hold the equivalent of one to two tampons. After wearing, rinse them in cold water, then toss them in the wash. These are simple, comfortable, and eco-friendly, though you'll need several pairs to get through your cycle.

Caring for the Environment

Reusable options like menstrual cups and period underwear are more sustainable and produce less waste compared to traditional pads and tampons, which often contain plastic and take hundreds of years to decompose. If you prefer disposable products, look for organic cotton options, which are free from harmful chemicals and gentler on the earth. Small changes in your period product choices can make a big impact on the environment over time.

Staying Safe and Comfortable

Safety is key when using period products. Tampons come with a rare risk of Toxic Shock Syndrome (TSS), so change them every 4–8 hours and use the lowest absorbency you need. With pads, cups, and period underwear, the risk of health issues is minimal.

Comfort is equally important. If a product doesn't feel right, try a different size or style until you find what works best for you. Everyone's body is different, so don't be afraid to experiment.

2.3 DISPOSING OF PERIOD PRODUCTS THOUGHTFULLY

Proper disposal of period products is essential for hygiene and respect for others. Here's how to do it neatly:

Pads and Panty Liners

- Peel it off your underwear and fold it in half with the sticky side out to keep things tidy.
- Wrap it in the product's wrapper, toilet paper, or a small disposal bag.
- Toss it in the trash—never flush pads or liners, as they can clog plumbing.

Tampons

- Remove the tampon and wrap it in toilet paper or a disposal bag.
- Throw it in the trash—don't flush it, as tampons can block pipes and harm the environment.

Period Underwear or Reusable Pads

- Place used items in a wet bag or container until you can wash them.
- Rinse them in cold water as soon as possible to prevent stains, then wash as directed.

Menstrual Cups

- Empty the cup into the toilet, rinse it with water, and reinsert.
- If you're in a public restroom, wipe it clean with toilet paper and wash it thoroughly later.

Be Kind: Clean Up After Yourself

It's normal to have a period, but it's also important to be considerate of others.

Always:

- Wrap used products neatly.
- Dispose of them properly—no one wants surprises!
- Wash your hands—no exceptions.

Taking a few extra seconds to clean up after yourself, it shows respect for yourself and those around you. Plus, it's just good manners!

It's normal to feel unsure about which product to use at first. Everyone is different, and what works for one person might not work for another. Don't worry about making the perfect choice right away. The important thing is to find something that makes you feel comfortable and confident. It's all about what feels right for you. As time goes on you will probably try the full variety of options as you get comfortable with your body and adapt to having your period.

Being prepared is the best way to feel confident about your period. As you are getting ready for your first-period's arrival, try on the pads, try several different sizes for ease and comfort while wearing them and try on the period panties, wear them. It will help you know how it will feel and bring about some comfort and familiarity when the big day arrives.

Note: Some cultures have restrictions on internal period products, such as tampons or menstrual cups; they are not allowed until after marriage.

2.4 THE PMS PUZZLE: UNDERSTANDING SYMPTOMS AND SOLUTIONS

Have you ever felt extra cranky or like your jeans are suddenly tighter for no reason? You might be experiencing PMS, which stands for premenstrual syndrome. It's a group of symptoms that some girls and women get before their period starts. These symptoms can vary widely. Some common physical symptoms include bloating, where you feel puffy or heavier than usual.

Cramps are another symptom. They feel like a tightness in your lower belly or back. Then there are the emotional symptoms. You might feel irritable, like everything is getting on your nerves. Or you might swing from happy to sad in a flash. These feelings are a normal part of PMS for many women. But not everyone will experience PMS the same way. Some girls might not feel anything at all, while others might have stronger symptoms.

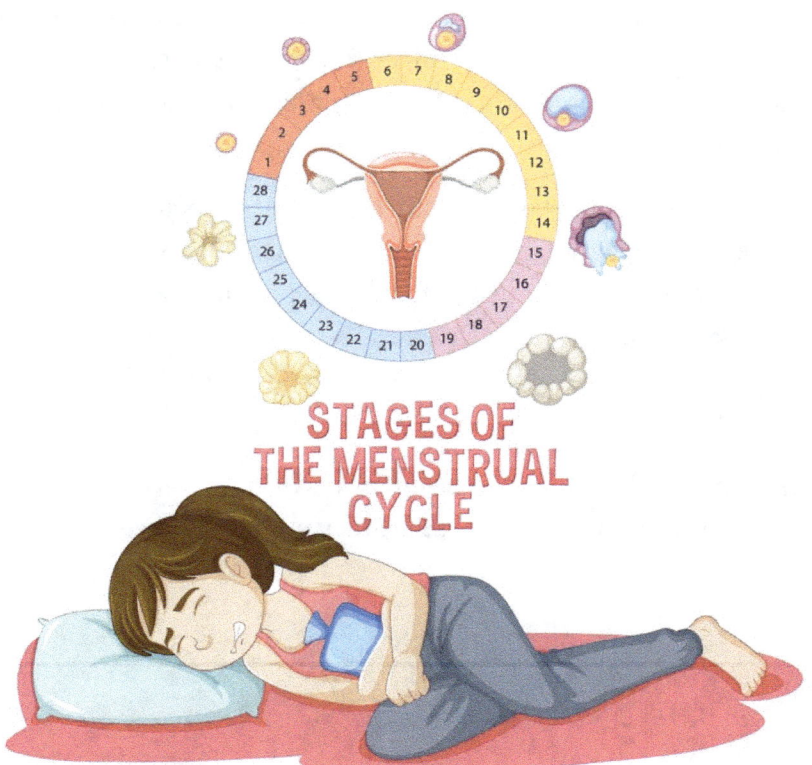

Finding ways to manage PMS can make a big difference in how you feel. One helpful strategy involves looking at what you eat. Eating foods rich in calcium, like yogurt or leafy greens, can ease some symptoms. Try to reduce salty snacks and caffeine, as they can make bloating worse. Drinking plenty of water helps too. Staying hydrated can actually reduce water retention and make you feel better. Adding exercise to your routine can also help. Activities like yoga or walking release endorphins, which are chemicals in your brain that make you feel good. Even a short walk can lift your mood and ease cramps. Relaxation techniques, such as deep breathing or listening to calming music, can also reduce stress and soothe your mind.Try a heating pad, hot water bottle, or a microwave warm pack for soothing cramps, too.

Talking about PMS with friends or family can be comforting. It helps to know you're not alone. Sharing your experiences can make them feel less overwhelming. You might discover that others have great tips for managing symptoms that you haven't tried yet. Sometimes, just saying how you feel out loud can make a big difference, knowing you are not alone. It's important to normalize talking about PMS, just like any other health topic. It's nothing to be embarrassed about. It's a natural part of life. By opening up, we help break down the stigma and make it easier for others to share too.

There are many myths about PMS that can be confusing. One common myth is that every girl gets PMS, but that's simply not true. Some girls never experience it. Others might only notice mild symptoms. Another myth is that PMS is an excuse for mood swings. While hormones do play a role in mood changes, they don't control your feelings completely. Your emotions are valid, and it's okay to feel them. Understanding and acknowledging PMS can help you manage it better. It's about finding what works best for you and making small changes to improve your well-being.

To make sense of what you're experiencing, keeping track of your symptoms can be helpful. Write down when you have them and how strong they are. This can help you see if there's a pattern. It can also be useful information to share with a doctor if you ever need medical advice. Remember, not every change in mood or body feeling is because of PMS. It's just one of many possibilities. Knowing your body and understanding what it needs can help you feel more in control and less out of sorts. Knowing the how's and why's goes a long way in helping you and cope with these new changes as you become a grown woman and start menstruating.

2.5 MANAGING PERIODS AT SCHOOL: TIPS AND TRICKS

Navigating your period while at school can feel like trying to keep a secret that everyone somehow already knows. But it doesn't have to be stressful. Planning ahead can make your day much smoother. Start by keeping spare supplies in your locker, backpack, or pencil case. Pack a few pads or tampons, some wipes, and even a spare pair of underwear. You might feel more relaxed knowing you have everything you need, just in case. When you feel your period coming, plan your bathroom breaks. Use break times between classes. It's the perfect chance to check everything is okay without rushing.

Sometimes, things don't go as planned. You might find yourself caught without supplies. Don't panic. All school nurses have period products. Many teachers are also understanding and willing to help.

If you worry about leaks, tie a sweater around your waist. It's a quick fix until you can change. You're not alone; others will understand and offer help if you ask. It's important to remember that everyone has moments of unpreparedness. It's just another part of life.

Creating a supportive environment at school is important. Talking to teachers or school nurses can help. They can offer advice or even make sure there are supplies in the bathrooms.

Encouraging a culture of support among classmates also helps. Start by talking to your friends. Share your experiences; it helps to know you are not alone but that you are in good company with the other girls facing the same challenges. You might find that they have tips to share, too. Understanding and support can make all the difference. A simple conversation can lead to a more inclusive and understanding community. You might even start a peer support group where you can talk openly and share experiences. Some girls may feel that sharing may not be as easy as others do, so be the trusted friend they can rely on and protect their privacy. These are the best kind of friends to have in your corner, the kind and supportive ones.

Participating in sports or gym class with your period might feel daunting. But you can still stay active and enjoy your favorite activities. Choose period products that fit your lifestyle. Tampons or menstrual cups are great for active days. They provide more freedom of movement. Period underwear is also a comfortable choice. It feels like regular underwear but offers added protection. Make sure you're comfortable. Wear dark, loose-fitting clothes for extra security. Staying active can actually help relieve cramps and improve your mood. Don't let your period hold you back from doing what you love.

Remember, having your period is a normal part of life. It doesn't have to stop you from enjoying your day at school. With a little preparation and support, you can manage it with ease. Whether it's keeping supplies handy, planning breaks, or leaning on friends, there are plenty of ways to make it work. You're capable of handling this, just like other girls do every day. Trust in yourself and your ability to manage it all.

2.6 PERIOD MYTHS BUSTED: SEPARATING FACT FROM FICTION

There's a lot of chatter about periods, and not all of it is true. Let's clear up some of the biggest myths out there. You might have heard that you can't swim while on your period. That's not true. Does your period stop when swimming? No, periods do not stop while swimming, but the water pressure can temporarily reduce or slow the flow. When you're submerged in water, such as in a pool, the water pressure can counteract the flow of blood, so you might notice little to no visible bleeding while swimming. However, once you're out of the water, the flow will resume as normal.

If you're worried about leaks while swimming, you can use tampons, menstrual cups, or specially designed period swimwear to stay comfortable and protected. These products are designed to work effectively even while you're active in the water. You can definitely swim. Wearing a tampon or a menstrual cup can help keep things tidy and comfortable in the water. These products are designed to stay in place and prevent leaks, so you can enjoy swimming just like any other day.

Another common myth is that periods should be painful. While some discomfort or cramps are normal, severe pain is not something you should just accept. It's important to talk to your mother/parent to help you talk with a doctor if your periods are very painful. They can help find ways to make you feel better.

There are also some strange ideas about menstruation itself. One is that having a period means you're sick. In reality, menstruation is a sign that your body is healthy and functioning as it should. It's part of the natural cycle that prepares your body for the possibility of pregnancy. It's not an illness, and it doesn't mean something is wrong. Another quirky myth is that if you and your friends spend a lot of time together, your periods  will sync up. This idea is called menstrual synchrony. While it's a fun thought, science has not yet proven it to be true. It's more likely that cycles overlap as just a coincidence. Each person's cycle is unique, and it follows its own rhythm.

It's important to question what you hear about periods. Not everything people say is based on facts. Encourage yourself to ask questions and seek out reliable information. Books, trusted adults, and healthcare professionals are great resources. If you come across something that sounds a bit strange, don't hesitate to look it up. Research helps you understand the truth about your body. Be curious and open to learning. By educating yourself, you can feel more confident and empowered about your period. It's all about replacing myths with facts.

Accurate knowledge about periods is powerful. It helps you make informed choices and reduces stigma. When you understand what's happening in your body, you can approach menstruation with confidence. This understanding also helps break down the shame some people feel about periods. There's nothing embarrassing about it. It's a natural part of life. By talking openly and sharing correct information, we can create a world where periods are no longer a taboo topic. We can celebrate them for what they are—a sign of life and growth.

As you move forward, remember that knowledge is your ally. It helps you make smart decisions and face challenges with courage. Embrace the facts, question what doesn't seem right, and always seek the truth. With the right information, you're ready to navigate anything.

3

EMOTIONAL ROLLERCOASTER

I magine you're at a birthday party with your closest friends. One moment, you're laughing so hard your sides hurt. The next, you feel an unexpected wave of sadness wash over you. It's confusing, right? You might wonder why your emotions are like a rollercoaster, with ups and downs that seem to come out of nowhere. But this is normal during puberty. Let's dive into why these mood swings happen and how you can navigate them.

Hormones are the main reason for these emotional changes. During puberty, your body starts producing more estrogen. This hormone can affect how you feel. Estrogen doesn't work alone, though. It teams up with neurotransmitters like serotonin. These are chemicals in your brain that help control your mood. Sometimes, the balance between estrogen and serotonin can get a little wobbly. This can make you feel happy one minute and irritable the next. It's like your brain is adjusting to a new rhythm. It might take some time to find a balance, but remember, you're not alone. Everyone goes through this, and it's just a part of growing up.

Mood swings can feel intense and unpredictable. It's important to know that emotional variability is normal. Think of your emotions like the weather. Sometimes it's sunny, and other times it's cloudy with a chance of rain. Just like the weather, your feelings can change, and that's okay. Many women all around you have experienced similar feelings at one time or another. Some women are more sensitive to the emotional mood swings than others, each of us are unique. Your mom, sister, aunt, grandma or even your teacher might have their own stories about mood swings during puberty. Hearing these stories can help you realize that what you're feeling is common. It's like being part of a club who understands what you're going through like Sophie's story.

Sophie slammed her bedroom door and flopped onto her bed, tears streaming down her face. She didn't even know why she was crying —it just felt like everything was wrong. Earlier that day, she had gotten into an argument with her best friend over something small. At lunch, she spilled juice on her new shirt, and to top it all off, her math teacher assigned extra homework. Now, even the sound of her little brother playing video games in the next room felt unbearable.

"Why am I like this?" Sophie muttered into her pillow. Her emotions felt like they were out of control—one moment she was happy, the next she was frustrated, and then the tears came rushing in. She hated feeling this way and didn't know what to do about it.

A soft knock came at her door. "Sophie, it's Mom. Can I come in?"

Sophie didn't answer, but after a moment, her mom pushed the door open gently and sat on the edge of her bed.

"What's going on, sweetheart?" her mom asked, stroking Sophie's hair.

"I don't know," Sophie sniffled. "I'm just... so mad and sad all the time! And I don't even know why!"

Her mom nodded knowingly. "It sounds like your hormones are in overdrive. This is totally normal, especially during puberty. Your body is changing a lot, and sometimes that means your emotions go a little haywire too."

Sophie looked up at her mom. "But I don't want to feel like this. I hate it."

"I know it's hard," her mom said softly. "But it's okay to have these feelings. You don't have to fight them or figure them out right away. What you can do is give yourself some grace. Take a deep breath and remind yourself it's okay to cry, to be upset, or even to just need some space."

Her mom pulled her into a hug. "And remember, you're never alone in this. I'm here anytime you need to talk or even just sit with you."

Sophie felt the tension in her chest start to ease. Her mom's words were like a balm, soothing the storm inside her. "Thanks, Mom," she whispered.

"Anytime, honey," her mom said with a smile. "Now, how about we make some hot chocolate and talk about your day? Or we can just sit together and watch a funny movie. Whatever you need."

Sophie nodded. "Hot chocolate sounds good."

As they headed to the kitchen, Sophie realized that even though her emotions were all over the place, it felt good to know she had someone who understood and loved her no matter what.

Managing these mood swings can help you feel more in control. One way to do this on your own is through deep breathing exercises. When you start feeling overwhelmed, take a moment to breathe deeply. Inhale through your nose, hold it for a few seconds, and then exhale slowly through your mouth. This can help calm your mind and body. Journaling is another great tool. Write down how you're feeling each day. It doesn't have to be perfect or make sense to anyone else. Just let your thoughts flow onto the paper. Over time, you might notice patterns in your emotions. This can help you understand what triggers certain feelings and how to handle them better.

It's also important to talk about your feelings. Sometimes, just saying what's on your mind can make you feel better. Find someone you trust, like a parent or guardian, and have a conversation. You might be surprised by how understanding they are. They can offer advice or just listen when you need to vent. Peer support groups can also be a great resource. These are spaces where you can meet others who are experiencing similar changes. Sharing your experiences and hearing others' stories can be comforting. It reminds you that you're not alone and that there are people who care.

Reflection Section: Mood Tracking Journal

- Take a notebook and create a mood journal.
- Write down how you feel each day. Include any events or thoughts that might have influenced your mood.
- After a few weeks, look for patterns. Are there certain times or situations that affect your emotions more?
- Use this information to help you prepare for and manage future mood swings.

Remember, puberty is a time of change, and it's okay to feel a bit all over the place. Your emotions are valid, and there's no right or wrong way to feel. The key is to find healthy ways to cope and reach out for support when you need it. You've got this!

3.1 STRESS LESS: COPING STRATEGIES FOR PUBERTY

Puberty can feel a bit like being in a pressure cooker. There are so many new things to deal with, and it's easy to feel stressed out. School can be a big part of that stress. You might have more home-work than ever before. Maybe there are tests that seem really hard. Teachers expect a lot from you, and it can feel like you have to be perfect all the time. Then there's the pressure from friends and social media. You might feel like you have to fit in or keep up with what everyone else is doing. These things can make you feel worried and overwhelmed. But guess what? There are ways to handle it all without letting stress take over your life.

One great way to manage stress is through mindfulness meditation. This is a simple practice where you focus on your breathing and stay present in the moment. Find a quiet space, close your eyes, and take slow deep breaths. Notice how your body feels and let your thoughts come and go without judging them. Even just a few minutes can help calm your mind and reduce stress. Another helpful skill is time management. This means planning out your tasks so you can stay on top of everything. Use a planner or calendar to write down your assignments and activities. Break big tasks into smaller ones and tackle them one at a time. It feels great to check things off your list, and it helps you avoid last-minute panic.

Exercise is also a wonderful way to relieve stress. Moving your body releases endorphins, which are chemicals that make you feel good. Yoga is perfect for relaxation. It combines gentle stretches with deep breathing. You don't have to be super flexible to try it. Start with simple poses like the tree pose or child's pose. If you enjoy being around others, consider joining a team sport. Playing soccer or basketball with friends isn't just fun, it's a great way to make new friends and support each other. The social interaction can boost your mood and help you forget about your worries, even if it's just for a little while.

Creative activities, using your hands and your mind can be a great distraction and can also help you express yourself and reduce stress. Grab some paper and start drawing or painting. You don't have to be an artist to enjoy it. Just let your imagination run wild. Use colors and shapes to show how you feel. Writing is another powerful outlet. Try writing a poem or short story. It doesn't matter if it rhymes or makes sense. Just put your thoughts and feelings on paper. Creating something new can give you a sense of accomplishment and joy. It's a chance to escape into your own world and leave your worries behind, even if just for a bit.

Creative Exercise: Stress Relief Art

- Find some paper, markers, or paints.
- Draw or paint something that represents how you feel today.
- Use colors that match your mood.
- Hang it up somewhere special as a reminder that you can handle anything.

Puberty comes with its own set of challenges, but learning how to manage stress can make a big difference. Remember, it's okay to feel stressed sometimes. It's all about finding what works for you and knowing you have the power to handle it. Whether it's through mindfulness, exercise, or creativity, there are many ways to keep stress in check.

3.2 BODY POSITIVITY: CELEBRATING YOUR UNIQUE SELF

Imagine standing in front of a mirror and seeing someone who's not quite who you expected. Maybe you're worried about a blemish or feeling like you don't quite match up to the images you see online. This is where body positivity comes in. It's about accepting and loving your body just the way it is. During puberty, your body changes in ways that can feel strange or even uncomfortable. But every change is a part of who you are becoming. Body positivity means celebrating all body types. It encourages you to embrace every new shape and size that comes with growing up. It's about understanding that beauty doesn't fit into one mold. It's diverse and includes everyone.

The media often tells us what beauty should look like. Social media, magazines, and TV shows can make it seem like there's only one way to be beautiful. But this isn't true. Beauty standards are often narrow and unrealistic. They don't reflect the amazing diversity of the real world. Challenge these ideas by thinking critically about what you see. Ask yourself if these images make you feel good or if they make you doubt yourself. Try to diversify your media consumption. Follow influencers and role models who celebrate different body types and backgrounds Look for people who inspire you and make you feel good about who you are. The more you see diverse beauty, the more you'll appreciate your unique self, like Mia is learning to do.

Mia stared at her reflection in the mirror, tugging at her shirt. She didn't like the way it fit. No matter how she stood, she couldn't make herself look like the girls she saw in magazines or on social media. Their bodies seemed perfect—flat stomachs, smooth skin, and long legs. Mia felt like she didn't measure up.

At school, it didn't help that some of her classmates casually commented on appearances. "She's so skinny; I wish I looked like her," one girl had said during lunch. Another replied, "Yeah, me too. I feel so fat."

Mia stayed quiet, but the words stuck in her mind. Was she supposed to look like that too? She started comparing herself to everyone—her friends, celebrities, even strangers. The more she thought about it, the worse she felt.

That night, Mia's mom noticed her unusually quiet mood. "What's on your mind, sweetie?" she asked.

Mia hesitated, then finally said, "Mom, why don't I look like the girls on Instagram? Everyone's so pretty, and I just feel... average."

Her mom sighed and sat down next to her. "Mia, the world can be really tough on girls when it comes to appearances. But those pictures you see? A lot of them aren't real. They're filtered, edited, and posed to look perfect. Even the people in those photos don't look like that in real life."

"But it's everywhere," Mia said. "How am I supposed to feel good about myself?"

Her mom smiled gently. "You're more than just what you see in the mirror. You have kindness, creativity, and strength—all things that make you beautiful. It's okay to want to take care of yourself, but don't let the world define your worth by looks alone."

Mia thought about her mom's words. It wasn't easy to ignore the pressure, but maybe she could start seeing herself differently—through her own eyes, not the world's lens.

As she got ready for bed, she looked at her reflection one more time. This time, instead of focusing on what she didn't like, she smiled and thought about what made her special. It was a small step, but it felt like the beginning of something important.

Self-love and acceptance can be nurtured through simple practices. Start each day with a positive affirmation. Stand in front of the mirror and tell yourself something kind. It might feel strange at first, but words have power. Saying, "I am beautiful just as I am" can change how you see yourself. Gratitude journaling is another way to focus on the positive. Write down three things you appreciate about your body. It could be your strong legs that carry you through the day or your bright smile that lights up a room. By focusing on what your body does for you, you'll start to appreciate it more. These small acts of self-care can make a big difference in how you feel.

There are countless stories of people who have embraced body positivity and found empowerment. Take, for example, a girl named Natasha. She always felt self-conscious about her height, often taller than her friends. But one day, she decided to join a basketball team. There, she found that her height was a strength, not a flaw. She embraced it and excelled in the sport she loved. Or consider the community movement that started in a local high school. Students came together to celebrate Body Positivity Day. They shared personal stories, wore outfits that made them feel confident, and created posters with messages of self-love. These stories show that embracing body positivity isn't just about feeling better about yourself. It's about finding strength in who you are and sharing that with others.

Empowerment Exercise: Daily Affirmation Challenge

- Each morning, stand in front of the mirror and say one positive thing about yourself.
- It can be about your appearance, a talent, or a personal achievement.
- Write it down on a note card, hang it on your mirror and reflect on how these affirmations make you feel over time.
- Remember you are fearfully and wonderfully made. There is no one exactly like you, you are unique! Just like you were created to be.

Body positivity is a powerful tool. It helps you see beyond the expectations and pressures of society. By accepting yourself and celebrating your uniqueness, you'll find a sense of peace and confidence. Remember, you're not alone in this. Young (and old) women all around the world are on the same path, working to embrace their true selves.

3.3 BUILDING CONFIDENCE: FINDING YOUR INNER STRENGTH

Confidence doesn't happen overnight. It's something you build, a little bit at a time. Think of it like planting a garden. You start with seeds, and over time, with care and attention, those seeds grow into strong plants. Supportive relationships are like the sun and rain that help your confidence grow. Having people in your life who believe in you can make a big difference. They remind you of your strengths when you forget them. They offer encouragement when you try new things. Reflecting on your experiences also helps. Take time to think about what makes you feel confident. Notice when you feel strong and what you were doing in those moments. This self-awareness is like a map that guides you on your way.

Exercise: Make a list of the positive people in your life- -the ones who cheer you on, believe in you and are always willing to help you. Examples like, your mom, aunt, grandma, neighbor, teacher, girlfriends, girlfriends mom,pastor's wife, etc. It's good to know who you have in your corner that you can call on when you need encouragement or help figuring out this journey of puberty. Having your squad can make it easier and even more fun!

Everyone has something special about them. That includes you. Maybe you're good at drawing, or perhaps you have a knack for solving puzzles. Whatever it is, recognizing your personal strengths is key to building confidence. Make a list of things you're good at. This is your strengths inventory. It can be anything, big or small. Maybe you're a great listener, or perhaps you're good at organizing things. Once you have your list, set some personal goals. If you love art, maybe your goal is to create a new drawing each week. Goals give you something to work towards and achieve. They help you grow your confidence, one step at a time.

Stepping out of your comfort zone can be scary, but it's a great way to build confidence. Trying new activities and challenges can show you just what you're capable of. Joining clubs or groups at school is a fantastic start. Whether it's drama club, the school newspaper, or a sports team, these activities help you discover new interests and skills. They can even help you identify what you don't like, and sometimes you just won't know unless you try it for yourself. This is the time of your life you are discovering new opportunities and adventures. Volunteering is another way to step up. It feels good to help others, and you learn a lot about yourself in the process. You might find that you have a talent for leadership or that you enjoy working as part of a team. Each new experience adds to your confidence.

Role models can be powerful guides on your confidence-building path. They show you what's possible and inspire you to keep going when things get tough. Think about people who you admire. Maybe it's a teacher who always encourages you, or a family member who has overcome challenges. These role models can show you how to stay strong. They can teach you about resilience and the power of persistence. Mentorship programs through your local church and community support initiatives can connect you with people who can guide you. They offer you a chance to learn from others' experiences and apply those lessons to your own life. Being part of a community that supports and believes in you is like having a team of cheerleaders by your side.

Confidence is something you build every day, with every choice you make and every positive step you take. It's about believing in yourself, even when things feel uncertain. It's knowing that you have the strength to try, to learn, and to grow. You have everything you need inside you. Sometimes, you just need a little reminder.

3.4 THE POWER OF POSITIVE SELF-TALK

Have you ever caught yourself thinking, "I'm just not good at this," or "I can't do it"? These thoughts can sneak in and make you doubt yourself. That's where positive self-talk comes in. It's the voice inside your head that encourages you, instead of bringing you down. Positive self-talk can change how you feel about yourself and the world around you. When you practice it, it boosts your self-esteem and makes you more resilient. It's like having a personal cheerleader in your mind, always rooting for you. Negative self-talk, on the other hand, is like a pesky gremlin that tries to convince you that you're not enough. But you have the power to change it with practice.

One way to start is by reframing negative thoughts. When you catch yourself thinking something unkind about yourself, stop and think about how you can turn it around. For example, if you think, "I messed up," try changing it to, "I learned something new." This small shift can help you see things in a more positive light. Visualization is another great technique. Close your eyes and picture yourself succeeding at something you want to achieve. It could be anything from acing a test to making a new friend. Imagine yourself feeling confident and happy. This practice helps your brain believe that you can do it. It's a bit like creating a mental movie where you're the star.

Affirmations and mantras can also play a big role in building positive self-talk. These are short, powerful statements you repeat to yourself. They help reinforce a positive mindset. Try saying, "I am capable and strong" when you need a boost of confidence. Or use "I embrace change and growth" when you face new challenges. These phrases remind you of your strengths and help ground you when things feel shaky. The more you say them, the more you believe them. It might feel silly at first, but stick with it. Over time, these words become a part of how you see yourself.

Making positive self-talk a daily habit is key to seeing its benefits. Start by setting aside a few minutes each day to practice. You can do this in front of a mirror, during a walk, or even as you get ready for bed. Track your progress by writing down your affirmations and how they make you feel. This reflection can help you see the changes in your mindset over time. Share your affirmations with friends, too. Encourage them to join you in this practice. You can swap affirmations and support each other in building a more positive outlook. It's amazing how a shared experience can strengthen friendships and create a supportive circle.

Exercise: Positive Affirmation Jar

- Find a small jar or box.
- Write down your favorite affirmations on slips of paper and put them in the jar. Examples: bible promise verses are great confidence builders,
- Each day, draw one out and focus on it. Repeat it to yourself throughout the day.
- Encourage friends to create their own jars and share their favorite affirmations with you.

Confidence-Building Affirmations and Quote Examples/Ideas

Positive Affirmations

I am capable of amazing things.

I deserve success and happiness.

I am confident in my abilities.

I am enough, just as I am.

I trust myself to make the right decisions.

I am worthy of love and respect.

I can achieve anything I set my mind to.

I am proud of how far I've come.

I am strong, resilient, and courageous.

I radiate confidence and positivity.

Motivational Quotes

Believe in yourself and all that you are. Know that there is something inside you that is greater than any obstacle.

— CHRISTIAN D. LARSON

Confidence comes not from always being right but from not fearing to be wrong.

— PETER T. MCINTYRE

The most beautiful thing you can wear is confidence.

— BLAKE LIVELY

Your potential is endless. Go do what you were created to do.

You are more powerful than you know; you are beautiful just as you are.

— MELISSA ETHERIDGE

Don't wait for confidence to take the next step. Take the step, and confidence will follow.

She believed she could, so she did.

— R.S. GREY

Act as if what you do makes a difference. It does.

— WILLIAM JAMES

Success is not final, failure is not fatal: it is the courage to continue that counts.

— WINSTON CHURCHILL

What lies behind us and what lies before us are tiny matters compared to what lies within us.

— RALPH

Faith-Based Affirmations

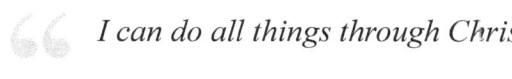

I can do all things through Christ who strengthens me.

— PHILIPPIANS 4:13

For I know the plans I have for you, declares the Lord, plans to prosper you and not to harm you, plans to give you hope and a future.

— JEREMIAH 29:11

God is within her; she will not fall.

— PSALM 46:5

I am fearfully and wonderfully made.

— PSALM 139:14

Be strong and courageous. Do not be afraid; do not be discouraged, for the Lord your God will be with you wherever you go.

— JOSHUA 1:9

<u>Short and Sweet Boosters</u>

I've got this!

I am unstoppable.

Every day is a fresh start.

I choose to see the best in myself.

Confidence looks good on me.

I have the power to create the life I want.

I am my own biggest cheerleader.

I am growing and evolving every day.

I am a magnet for positivity and success.

I am brave, bold, and beautiful.

Positive self-talk isn't just about words. It's about changing the way you think and feel. The more you think positively the more you'll believe and act with confidence. It's about building a mindset that supports you, no matter what life throws your way. By practicing regularly and sharing with others, you'll find that your inner voice becomes a source of strength and encouragement. You have the power to choose and shape your world.

3.5 DEALING WITH PEER PRESSURE: STAYING TRUE TO YOURSELF

Imagine you're hanging out with your friends, and someone suggests doing something you're not comfortable with. Maybe it's trying a new trend that doesn't feel right for you, or perhaps it's skipping school just because everyone else is doing it. This is peer pressure. It's what happens when you feel pushed to do something because others are doing it. Peer pressure can be direct, like when someone tells you to do something. It can also be indirect, where you feel like you have to follow along just to fit in. Social media can make peer pressure even stronger. You might see posts of people doing things that seem fun or cool, and it might make you feel like you need to do the same. But it's important to remember that you don't have to do anything that doesn't feel right for you.

Resisting peer pressure starts with knowing who you are and what you believe in. This means developing a strong sense of self. Think about what matters to you and what makes you comfortable. These are your values, and they guide your choices. Assertive communication is a helpful tool. It's about saying what you think and feel clearly and confidently. If someone asks you to do something you don't want to do, you can say, "No, I'm not interested," or "That's not for me." You don't have to explain or apologize. Just being firm and clear can help others understand your boundaries. Practice saying no in front of a mirror or with a friend. The more you do it, the easier it will get.

Here's how Sarah, a brave and confident girl, faced peer pressure at school. Her friends wanted her to skip class and hang out at the mall. Sarah thought about what was important to her and decided to stand her ground. She told her friends she had a test she wanted to study for and suggested meeting up after school instead. At first, her friends teased her. But eventually, they respected her decision. Sarah learned that staying true to herself felt better than going along with something she didn't want to do. She also realized that her true friends supported her choices. This experience helped Sarah grow stronger and more confident in her decisions.

Building a supportive network can help you resist peer pressure. Surround yourself with people who respect your boundaries and support your choices. Choose friends who share your values and encourage you to be yourself. It's easier to stand firm when you have others by your side who understand and respect you. Engaging in group activities that align with your values can also help. Join clubs or teams where you meet people who enjoy the same things as you. Whether it's drama club, a sports team, or a book club, these groups can offer a sense of belonging and support. They help you stay focused on what matters to you and remind you that you're not alone.

When you face peer pressure, remember that you have the power to make your own choices. It's okay to say no and to stand up for what you believe in. You don't have to follow the crowd, especially if it doesn't feel right for you. Staying true to yourself is more important than fitting in with others. By being confident in your values and surrounding yourself with supportive friends, you can navigate peer pressure and stay true to who you are.

SELF-CARE AND WELLNESS

Picture this: it's a Monday morning, and you're rushing to get ready for school. You grab your backpack, your lunch, and head for the door. But wait, did you remember to brush your teeth? Did you wash your face? These small steps might seem like just another thing to do, but they are super important. They help keep you healthy and feeling good. Self-care is all about taking care of your body and mind. It's about making sure you feel your best every day. Let's dive into some simple ways to keep yourself fresh and clean.

Staying fresh starts with a simple daily routine. Taking a shower or bath each day is a great way to wash away sweat and dirt. Especially during puberty, as your body changes. You might notice you sweat more or that your skin gets oily. Bathing helps manage these changes. Use a mild soap to clean your body. It helps keep your skin healthy without causing irritation. After showering, put on clean clothes. This helps you feel comfortable and confident. Handwashing is another key part of hygiene. You touch so many things every day. Washing your hands regularly helps prevent the spread of germs. Make sure to wash your hands before eating, after using the bathroom, and whenever they look dirty. Use warm water and soap. Scrub all parts of your hands, including between your fingers, for at least 20 seconds. Singing "Happy Birthday" twice is a fun way to make sure you're washing long enough.

Dealing With Body Odor

Managing body odor is important too. During puberty, sweat glands become more active. This can lead to body odor, especially under your arms. Deodorants can help, there are many varieties to choose from, it is wise to read labels and ingredients and find the best option for your needs. It could be that you prefer a certain smell or fragrance, or it could be that you want an unscented option. There are different applications for deodorant, like roll-ons, solid sticks, creams, salt stones, and sprays of different sorts. They mask the smell of sweat and keep you feeling fresh.

Antiperspirants go a step further. They reduce the amount of sweat your body produces. Choose a product that feels good on your skin. Wearing breathable fabrics like cotton also helps. These fabrics let your skin breathe and reduce sweating.

Oral hygiene is just as important as body hygiene. Brushing your teeth twice a day keeps your mouth healthy. Use a toothbrush with soft bristles and fluoride toothpaste. Brush all surfaces of your teeth and your tongue. This removes food particles and plaque. Flossing once a day is also key. It reaches places your toothbrush can't. Regular dental check-ups are important too. They help catch any problems early, keeping your smile bright and healthy. Many Tweens are also getting braces at this time for aligning their bite and straightening their teeth. Regular brushing and flossing are essential to preventing cavities and decay.

Your skin is your body's largest organ, and it needs care too. Washing your face every morning and night is a good start. Use a gentle cleanser to remove dirt and oil. Avoid products with harsh chemicals. They can irritate your skin. After cleansing, apply a moisturizer. It keeps your skin hydrated and smooth. Look for non-comedogenic products. They won't block your pores, which helps prevent acne. If you wear makeup, make sure to remove it before bed. It allows your skin to breathe and rejuvenate to stay healthy and clean.

Obvious acne   Washing face

Greasy hair   shampooing hair

Reflection Exercise: My Daily Routine Checklist

- Make a plan for your daily hygiene routine, to make it a new habit.
- Include steps like showering, handwashing, and brushing your teeth.
- Check off each task as you complete it.
- Reflect on how these habits make you feel throughout the day.

Taking care of yourself is important. It helps you feel good inside and out. These simple habits can make a big difference in your health and confidence. You deserve to look and feel your best every day!

4.1 NUTRITION FOR A GROWING BODY: WHAT TO EAT DURING PUBERTY

Imagine your body as a growing plant. Just like a plant needs sunlight and water, your body needs the right nutrients to grow and thrive. During puberty, everything is changing and developing. This makes nutrition super important. Balanced meals give your body the energy and nutrients it needs. Think of your plate as a rainbow. Fill it with a variety of foods to make sure you're getting all the necessary vitamins and minerals. Colorful fruits and vegetables provide vitamins like A and C. Whole grains give you energy that lasts through the day. Proteins like chicken, beans, or tofu help build strong muscles.

Vitamins and minerals play a big role in keeping your body healthy. Calcium and iron are especially important during this time. Calcium helps your bones grow strong. You can find it in foods like leafy greens, milk, and cheese. Iron supports your body by making red blood cells, which carry oxygen. Foods rich in iron include spinach and lean meats. Without enough iron, you might feel tired or weak. Don't forget about zinc and magnesium. They help with growth and energy. You can get them from nuts, seeds, and whole grains.

Nutrient-rich foods are like super fuel for your body. Leafy greens like kale and broccoli are packed with calcium and iron. They're great for keeping your bones and blood healthy. Whole grains like brown rice and oats give your body energy that lasts. They help keep you full and focused throughout the day. Snack on nuts and seeds for a boost of healthy fats and protein. They're perfect for when you need a quick pick-me-up after school or between activities. And, don't forget fruits. They're full of vitamins and make a sweet, healthy treat.

Water is just as important as the food you eat. Staying hydrated helps your body function properly. It keeps your skin clear, aids digestion, and helps you concentrate better. Aim to drink about eight glasses of water a day. This might seem like a lot, but it helps keep you feeling your best. Carry a water bottle with you to school. Sip on it throughout the day to stay hydrated. Listen to your body's cues. If you feel thirsty, your body is asking for water. Signs of dehydration include feeling tired, having a dry mouth, or getting a headache. If you notice these, take a break and have a drink.

Eating mindfully means listening to your body. It's about knowing when you're hungry and when you've had enough. Pay attention to hunger and fullness signals. Eat slowly and enjoy each bite. This helps you recognize when you're full and prevents overeating. It's easy to eat quickly when you're busy or distracted. But taking time to eat can help you enjoy your meal more. Avoid eating out of boredom or stress. These emotions can lead to unhealthy eating habits. Instead, find other ways to manage your feelings, like talking to a friend or going for a walk.

Making healthy food choices during puberty sets the foundation for a strong and healthy life. Your body is working hard to grow and change, and it needs the right fuel to do so. Eating a balanced diet full of nutrients helps you feel energized and ready to take on whatever comes your way.

4.2 SLEEP MATTERS: THE IMPORTANCE OF RESTFUL NIGHTS

Imagine snuggling into your cozy bed after a long day. You close your eyes, and soon you drift off into a world of dreams. But sleep is more than just about dreams. It's when your body does some of its most important work. During sleep, your body releases hormones that are key for growth and healing. These hormones help your muscles grow, repair cells, and boost your immune system. It's like your body's nightly tune-up. Sleep also plays a big role in taking care of your brain. It helps you focus and learn better. When you get enough sleep, you can think clearly and remember things more easily. A good night's sleep can also make you feel happier and less stressed.

Getting into a good sleep routine can help you enjoy all these benefits. Try to go to bed and wake up at the same time every day, even on weekends. This helps your body get into a rhythm that makes falling asleep easier. Creating a bedtime routine can also signal to your body that it's time to wind down. You can start by dimming the lights and doing something relaxing. Think of reading a book or listening to calming music. It's like telling your body, "Hey, it's time to relax." Avoid exciting activities like playing video games or watching action-packed shows right before bed. These can make it harder to fall asleep.

Sometimes, falling asleep can feel like trying to catch a slippery fish. One way to make it easier is to limit your screen time before bed. The blue light from phones and tablets can trick your brain into thinking it's still daytime. Try to turn off screens at least an hour before you want to sleep. If you find yourself tossing and turning, try some relaxation techniques. Take slow, deep breaths. Inhale deeply and then exhale slowly. Picture a peaceful place, like a beach or a forest. This can help calm your mind. If your thoughts keep racing, jot them down in a notebook. Sometimes, writing things down can help clear your mind.

Quality sleep can help you shine in your daily life. When you're well-rested, you're ready to tackle schoolwork and activities with energy and focus. You might find it easier to concentrate in class or remember what you studied. Sleep also helps with emotional balance. It's easier to handle stress and emotions when you've had enough rest. You might find you're more patient and less likely to feel overwhelmed. It's like having a superpower that helps you stay calm and cool.

Getting enough sleep is a simple way to take care of yourself. It helps your body grow, keeps your brain sharp, and makes you feel good. By setting a bedtime routine and creating a relaxing environment, you can enjoy all the benefits of a good night's sleep.

4.3 EXERCISE AND MOVEMENT: STAYING ACTIVE FOR HEALTH

You know that feeling of running across a field, wind in your hair, the world blurring around you? It's not just fun; it's great for your body too. Running, swimming, and other cardiovascular activities are like powerful engines for your heart and lungs. They keep everything working smoothly. They help your heart pump blood better and make your lungs stronger. Plus, they're a great way to burn off energy. You might not notice it right away, but these activities also help you focus better. They give your brain a boost, making it easier to tackle homework or concentrate in class. So next time you're out running around, know that you're doing something amazing for yourself.

But it's not just about running. Strength training is important too. And you don't need fancy gym equipment to get started. Your own body weight is all you need. Think of exercises like push-ups, sit-ups, or planks. These help build muscle and make your bones stronger. Strong muscles support your joints and help prevent injuries. They also help you carry your backpack more easily. Building strength isn't just about being strong. It's about feeling strong, inside and out. You'll notice you feel more confident when you know your body can handle whatever comes its way.

Staying active is great for your mind too. Exercise helps reduce stress and anxiety. When you move, your body releases chemicals called endorphins. These are like little happiness boosters. They make you feel calm and happy. Try moving a bit every day. It doesn't have to be much. Even walking or biking to school counts. It's a simple way to fit exercise into your routine. If you're looking for something more social, team sports or dance classes are perfect. They let you move and have fun with others. It's a win-win!

Finding activities you love is key. When you enjoy what you're doing, it doesn't feel like a chore. It feels like play. Explore different options to see what makes you happy. Maybe you'll find joy in yoga, where you can stretch and relax at the same time. Or martial arts might be your thing, offering a mix of discipline and movement. Community sports leagues offer a great way to try something new. They often welcome players of all levels, so you can learn and grow with others.

If you're not sure where to start, think about what makes you smile when you move. Is it dancing around your room to your favorite song? Is it playing tag with friends at the park? Whatever it is, make time for it. Moving your body should feel good. It's your chance to explore what you love and what your body can do.

Exercise isn't just about staying in shape. It's about feeling good and taking care of yourself. It's about creating a habit that supports your body and mind. So lace up those sneakers, grab your bike, or roll out your mat. Movement is your friend, and it's waiting for you to join in.

4.4 MINDFULNESS AND RELAXATION TECHNIQUES

Imagine sitting under a tree on a sunny day, feeling the gentle breeze and listening to birds chirping. That sense of peace and being present in the moment is what mindfulness is all about. It's a way to help you manage stress and emotions. When life feels overwhelming, mindfulness can bring you back to a calm place. It helps you focus on the present, not the past or future. By practicing mindfulness, you can reduce anxiety and feel more relaxed. It's like hitting the pause button on your busy life, giving you space to breathe and think clearly.

Mindfulness can start with something as simple as breathing. Deep breathing exercises are a great way to begin. Find a quiet spot, sit comfortably, and close your eyes. Take a slow, deep breath in through your nose. Hold it for a moment, then slowly exhale through your mouth. As you breathe out, imagine letting go of any stress or worries. Do this a few times, focusing only on your breath. It's a small step, but it can make a big difference in how you feel. Another technique is guided imagery. Picture a peaceful scene, like a beach or forest. Imagine yourself there, feeling the warmth of the sun or hearing the rustle of leaves. This visualization can help shift your mind from stress to serenity.

Finding emotional balance can be tricky, but relaxation methods can help. Progressive muscle relaxation is an effective way to release tension. Start by tensing the muscles in your feet, holding for a few seconds, then slowly relaxing them. Work your way up your body, tightening and relaxing each muscle group. This exercise helps you become aware of where you hold tension and how to let it go. Listening to calming music or nature sounds also promotes relaxation. Choose music that soothes you, like gentle piano melodies or the sound of rain. Close your eyes and let the sounds wash over you, taking you to a peaceful place. These activities can help you find calm, even on the busiest days.

The key to mindfulness is regular practice. Setting aside a little time each day can make it a natural part of your routine. It doesn't have to be long. Even just five or ten minutes can be effective. Find a time that works for you, like in the morning before school or right before bed. Consistency is important. It helps you build a habit that can benefit you in many areas of your life, starting now and into your future. Keeping a journal of your mindfulness practice can also help. Write down how you feel before and after each session. Note any changes in your mood or stress levels. It's a great way to track your progress and see the benefits over time.

Mindfulness Exercise: Breathing and Visualization

- Find a quiet place to sit comfortably.
- Close your eyes and take three slow, deep breaths.
- Picture a peaceful scene in your mind. It could be a beach, forest, or favorite memory, whatever makes you feel calm.
- Spend a few minutes exploring this place in your mind, using your senses. Feel the sand, hear the waves, or smell the pine trees.
- Slowly bring your focus back to the present, open your eyes, and notice how you feel.

Mindfulness and relaxation are tools you can use anytime, anywhere. They help you connect with yourself and find peace amidst the chaos. With practice, they can become part of your daily life, helping you handle stress with ease.

4.5 CREATING A SELF-CARE ROUTINE: YOUR PERSONAL GUIDE

Self-care is one of those things that sounds simple but can make a big difference in how you feel. It's about taking a little time to focus on yourself, away from the hustle and bustle of everyday life. During puberty, everything seems to be changing. Your body, your emotions, and even your friendships. It's easy to get caught up in all the noise. That's why self-care is so important. It helps you prioritize your own needs and wellness. It's like giving yourself a little love and attention, which you totally deserve. Think of it as a way to recharge your batteries so you can take on the world with energy and confidence.

Creating a self-care routine means finding activities that make you feel good. Start by thinking about what you enjoy. Maybe it's reading a book under a cozy blanket or writing your thoughts in a journal. You might like taking a walk in the park or spending time with a pet. These activities are more than just hobbies. They are ways to connect with yourself and feel at ease. Once you have a list of things you love, schedule some time for them. It doesn't have to be a lot. Even fifteen minutes a day can make a difference. Put it on your calendar like an appointment, and stick to it. This is your time to focus on you.

Experimentation is key. What works today might not work tomorrow. Your needs can change, and that's okay. Be open to trying new things. Maybe you'll discover that painting relaxes you or that weight-lifting helps you feel centered. If something doesn't feel right, it's okay to change it up. Self-care is personal and should fit your life, not the other way around. Flexibility is important. As you grow, your interests and needs will evolve. Let your routine grow with you. It's a bit like finding the right shoes. Sometimes you need to try on a few pairs of shoes to find the perfect fit. And just like you wear different shoes for different activities, you'll also find different routines and self-care options as you grow-up.

There are so many ways to practice self-care. Reading can transport you to other worlds and give your mind a break. Journaling lets you pour out your thoughts and feelings, helping you understand them better. Spending time in nature is another wonderful way to practice self-care. Take a walk in the woods or sit by a lake. Let the sounds and sights around you bring you peace. If you have a pet, spend time playing or cuddling with them. Animals have a special way of making us feel loved and happy. Whatever you choose, make sure it's something that brings you joy.

Self-care is not about being selfish. It's about knowing that you matter and that taking care of yourself is important. It's about recognizing when you need a break and giving yourself permission to take it. Life can be busy and demanding. But when you make self-care a priority, you're actually giving yourself the strength to handle it all. It's a way to say, "I am important, and I deserve to feel good. Be kind to yourself and make it a priority to find rest and activities that bring balance and joy to your life.

As we wrap up our chapter on self-care and wellness, keep in mind that these practices are part of a bigger picture. They help you grow into a healthy, happy version of yourself. As you move forward, remember that self-care is an ongoing process. It's about finding what works for you and making it a part of your life. Next, we will explore how to navigate social situations, which can be tricky but are an important part of growing up.

Hi there, Amazing Reader!

Are you enjoying *The Essential Girl's Guide to Puberty & Periods: Ages 8-14* so far? Your feedback means the world to me and helps other readers discover this book.

If you're finding the content helpful, inspiring, or just plain fun, I'd be incredibly grateful if you could take a moment to share your thoughts in an Amazon review. It doesn't have to be long—just a few sentences about what you like most would make a big difference!

It Only Takes a Moment

Scan the QR code to leave your review and share how this book made a difference for you or your family:

Thank you for being part of this journey and for supporting my work. Happy reading!

Warmly,

DebbieAnn

5

NAVIGATING SOCIAL SITUATIONS

P icture this: it's the first day of a new school year, and you walk into the lunchroom. You're holding your tray, scanning the room for familiar faces, hoping to spot a friend. Finding your place in social settings can be like solving a puzzle. Each piece represents a different part of what makes a good friend, and putting them together helps create strong connections. Friendships are super important. They offer support when things get tough and share in your victories when things go right. But how do you build these lasting connections? Let's dive into what makes a friendship healthy and supportive.

A good friend is like a cozy blanket on a chilly day. They offer warmth and comfort and make you feel safe. Trust is the foundation. You need to know you can share secrets without them being shared. Honesty is just as important. Being truthful with each other builds a strong bond. Respect and understanding keep the friendship balanced. It means listening to each other's ideas, even when you don't agree. It also means accepting your friend's quirks and differences.

A supportive friend encourages you to grow. They cheer you on and celebrate your victories.

Making new friends might seem daunting, but it's not as hard as it seems. Joining clubs or activities is a great way to meet people who share your interests. Whether it's drama club or a soccer team, these groups offer a chance to connect over common goals. Regular communication is key. Check-in with your friends, even if it's just a quick text or a funny meme. These small gestures show you care. Remember, friendships need nurturing. Like a plant that needs water and sunlight, friendships thrive with attention and effort.

Every friendship has its bumps. Misunderstandings happen, but they don't have to end a friendship. Effective listening is a powerful tool. It means really hearing what your friend is saying, not just waiting for your turn to talk. Show empathy by putting yourself in their shoes. Apologizing when you're wrong is important too. It shows you care about the friendship more than being right. Forgiveness goes hand in hand with apologizing. Holding onto grudges weighs down a friendship. Letting go can open the door to healing and growth. Misunderstandings handled well can strengthen a friendship with honesty and truth, it can also strengthen your relationship in trustworthiness. A trusted friend is a priceless treasure.

Boundaries are like invisible lines that keep friendships healthy. They set limits on what feels comfortable. It's okay to say no to things that don't feel right. Maybe your friend wants to borrow something you're not ready to share, or they suggest doing something you're not comfortable with. Saying no is part of respecting your own needs. It's also important to understand and accept differences. Not every friend will think or act the same way you do, and that's okay. Embracing these differences can make the friendship stronger.

Reflection Exercise: Friendship Map

- Draw a map of your current friendships.
- Write down what you appreciate about each friend.
- Identify any areas where you can improve, like communication or setting boundaries.
- Use this map to guide how you nurture and grow your friendships.

Friendships are like gardens. They need care, attention, and sometimes a little weeding to keep them healthy. By understanding what makes a good friend and how to nurture these bonds, you can build lasting relationships that support and uplift you.

5.1 SOCIAL MEDIA SAVVY: NAVIGATING THE DIGITAL WORLD

Social media can feel like a huge part of life. It's where we share pictures, comment on posts, and keep up with friends. It lets you stay connected with people, even if they live far away. You can chat with a friend who moved to another city or see what your cousin across the country is up to. It makes the world feel smaller and brings people closer together. But there's another side to it. Sometimes, scrolling through social media can make you feel like you're not quite measuring up. You might see your friend's perfect vacation photos or a classmate's amazing new outfit and start to compare yourself to these polished images. Remember, these pictures often show only the best moments. They don't tell the whole story. Everyone has ups and downs, even if they don't post about them. And remember this, most people never post things that make them look bad or out of sorts. So, when you are comparing your bad day to those posts it is not reality and you are in an unfair challenge to measure yourself against them.

Using social media safely is impor-tant. It starts with understanding privacy settings. These settings control who can see your posts or send you messages. Make sure you know how to adjust them so you feel comfortable. You might want to keep certain things private, sharing only with close friends or family. It's also good to know how to recog-nize and report inappropriate content. If you see something that  makes you feel uncomfortable or unsafe, like bullying or harass-ment, report it. Most platforms have tools for this. They help keep social media a safer space for everyone. Trust your instincts. If something doesn't feel right, it's okay to take action or ask for help from your parents, guardian, teacher, trusted adult, etc.

Taking breaks from social media can be refreshing. Sometimes, it feels like there's pressure to always be online, but it's healthy to step back now and then. Plan some offline time. Go for a walk, read a book, or spend time with friends face-to-face. These activities help you recharge and enjoy the world around you. You might find you're more relaxed and focused when you're not constantly checking your phone. Engaging in face-to-face interactions also strengthens your real-life connections. It's fun to share a laugh in person or have a deep conversation without the distraction of notifications. These moments make friendships more meaningful and lasting.

Digital empathy means being kind and thoughtful online. Words have power, even on a screen. It's easy to forget that there's a real person on the other side of a comment or message. Avoid negative comments and cyberbullying. Instead, focus on spreading positivity. If a friend posts about a tough day, send them an encouraging message. Let them know you are there for them.

Supporting friends through positive messages can brighten their day. It also makes social media a better place for everyone. Remember, a kind word can go a long way. It shows you care and helps build a community where everyone feels safe and respected.

5.2 CRUSHES AND FIRST LOVES: UNDERSTANDING ROMANTIC FEELINGS

Do you remember the first time you felt butterflies in your stomach when someone special walked into the room? It's a feeling like no other. Crushes and first loves often begin with a simple glance or a smile that makes your heart race. During puberty, romantic feelings start to develop, bringing with them a mix of excitement and curiosity. You might find yourself daydreaming about that person, imagining what it would be like to spend more time together. These feelings can be intense. They might even seem a bit overwhelming at times. It's perfectly normal. Infatuation is a powerful emotion that can make everything else fade into the background.

It's important to handle these feelings responsibly. Recognizing boundaries is a key part of this. Everyone has their own comfort levels, and it's important to respect them. This means taking things slow and making sure both people feel comfortable with how the relationship is going. It's also important to remember your friendships. When you're caught up in the excitement of a new crush, it's easy to lose sight of your other relationships. Balancing time between girlfriends and a new crush is important. Your friends are there for you, and they want to share in your happiness. Make sure to include them in your life, even when you're wrapped up in romance.

There are a lot of misconceptions about romance, especially from what we see in movies and on TV. Hollywood often shows relationships as perfect and easy. But real-life relationships require effort and understanding. They aren't always like the fairy tales we see on screen. It's important to have realistic expectations. Crushes can be temporary. Feelings might fade, and that's okay. It's all part of discovering what you like and who you connect with. Experiencing different feelings helps you learn more about what you want in a relationship. It's a process that helps you grow.

Here's the story of my first crush. It all happened so fast. I was a junior bridesmaid in my Aunt's wedding. His name was Travis. He lived on the east coast and I lived on the west coast. He and his family came in for the wedding and we had never met before. It was just that one day, we walked the aisle together, sat together at dinner with the bridal party, and danced all night long. It felt like true love. Then the night was over. I never saw him again, or had any way to connect since there wasn't social media in those days. It was a whirlwind of emotions for an almost 10 year old girl.

Talking about your feelings can be incredibly helpful. It's good to share what you're going through with someone you trust. Parents and guardians can offer wisdom and support. They've been through it before and can help guide you. Older siblings or mentors can also be great sources of advice. They can share their experiences and help you make sense of your own feelings. Opening up might feel a bit scary at first, but it can bring relief. Knowing that others understand what you're going through makes it easier to navigate the ups and downs of romance. Sharing your feelings doesn't mean you have to have all the answers. It's about having someone to listen and support you.

Crushes and first loves are part of growing up. They are filled with wonderful moments and learning experiences. Embrace these feelings. They help you understand yourself better and build connections with others. It's a journey of discovery, one that shapes who you are and who you want to become.

5.3 HANDLING BULLYING AND TEASING: STANDING UP FOR YOURSELF

Imagine walking down the hallway at school, and someone makes a mean comment about your new haircut. It stings. You might wonder why people can be so hurtful. Bullying and teasing can feel overwhelming, but understanding what they are can help you deal with them. Bullying is when someone uses power to hurt or control another person. It can be verbal, like name-calling, physical, like shoving, or even cyberbullying, which happens online. Teasing might start off as playful, but it can quickly turn into bullying if it becomes mean or relentless. It affects how you feel about yourself and your safety. Knowing the difference helps you know how to respond and seek help.

Facing bullies isn't easy, but there are ways to stand up for yourself. Assertive communication is one technique. It means speaking up clearly and confidently. If someone is teasing you, you can say, "I don't like that. Please stop." It lets the bully know you're not going to accept their behavior. Remember, being assertive is different from being aggressive. It's about standing your ground without being mean in return. If the situation doesn't improve, it's important to seek help. Talk to a teacher or school counselor. They're there to support you and can help stop the bullying. Sometimes, it might feel like you should handle it on your own, but asking for help shows strength.

Building a support network is important. Surround yourself with friends who care about you. They can stand by you and offer comfort when things get tough. Together, you can create a space where everyone feels safe and respected. Engaging in group activities, like clubs or sports, can also help. These groups can offer protection and camaraderie, making it harder for bullies to target you. Having a circle of friends means you're never alone. They can walk with you in the hallways or eat lunch with you, creating a sense of belonging. It's empowering to know that others have your back and in turn you have their back, too.

Self-empowerment and resilience are like shields against bullying. They help you build confidence and strength. Developing a strong sense of self-worth is key. Remind yourself of your strengths and what makes you unique. Practicing positive affirmations can help. Start each day by looking in the mirror and saying something kind to yourself, like, "I am strong and worthy." These words help you believe in yourself. When you know your value, it's easier to brush off hurtful comments. You become more resilient and able to bounce back from challenges with grace and courage.

Bullying and teasing can leave scars, but they don't have to define you. By learning to stand up for yourself, seeking support, and building confidence, you can navigate these challenges. Remember, you're not alone. There are people who care about you and want to help. You have the power to overcome bullying and grow stronger from it. Keep reaching out, finding allies, and believing in yourself. Your voice matters, and you deserve to be heard and respected.

5.4 COMMUNICATING WITH PARENTS AND GUARDIANS

Picture this: you've had a long day at school, filled with new experiences and big feelings. You come home, and your parent or guardian asks how your day was. It's tempting to just say, "Fine," and head to your room. But there's so much more beneath the surface. Talking with parents or guardians can be a bit like opening a window. It lets fresh air in and helps you see things more clearly. Open communication is key during puberty. It helps build trust and understanding. Sharing your experiences and feelings can bring you closer and make life's changes easier to handle.

Finding the right time and setting for these conversations makes a world of difference. Look for a moment when everyone is relaxed, like during a family meal or a quiet evening at home. This sets the stage for a meaningful chat. Using "I" statements can help express your feelings without sounding like you're blaming anyone. For example, say, "I felt overwhelmed at school today," instead of, "You never understand my school problems." This approach keeps the focus on your feelings and invites your parent to listen and support you. It's not always easy, but these small changes in how you talk can make the conversation smoother.

Sometimes it seems like there's a wall between you and your parents. Misunderstandings happen. Maybe they don't quite get what you're going through, or they have their own ideas about how things should be. Finding common ground is important. Listen to their perspective and share yours, too. Compromise can be a powerful tool. It's like meeting in the middle. For example, if you want more independence, suggest a way to earn their trust, like completing chores or improving your grades. This shows you're willing to work together and respect their concerns.

Communication is a two-way street, and building a bridge takes effort from both sides.

Having your parents involved during puberty can be comforting. They've been through similar changes and can offer guidance based on their experiences. Don't hesitate to ask for advice on personal issues, whether it's about friendships, school, or feelings. Involving them in decision-making processes can also be helpful. Say you're deciding whether to join a new club or try out for a team. Discussing the pros and cons with them can provide valuable insights. They might offer support you hadn't considered. Knowing you have someone on your side can boost your confidence and help you make informed choices.

Growing up brings a whirlwind of changes. You don't have to face them alone. Your parents or guardians are there to help you navigate the twists and turns. They want the best for you. Even when it feels like they're being overprotective, it's usually because they care deeply. They can see ahead because of their own choices or experiences at your age and want to help you navigate your decisions and feelings. By keeping the lines of communication open, you create a space for honesty and understanding. It's a safe place where you can share your triumphs and challenges without fear of judgment. Over time, these conversations strengthen your relationship. They build a solid foundation of trust and support that you can rely on.

5.5 FINDING YOUR VOICE: SPEAKING UP AND BEING HEARD

Finding your voice is like discovering a hidden treasure within yourself. It's about recognizing the power of your thoughts and the importance of sharing them with others. Speaking up in class or in a group setting can feel nerve-wracking, but it's a skill worth practicing. Imagine raising your hand in class and sharing an idea that's been brewing in your mind. It's a moment of courage, and it shows that you value your own opinions. Your voice matters, and expressing your thoughts can inspire others. When you speak with confidence, it signals to others that you believe in what you're saying, and it encourages them to listen.

To express yourself clearly and respectfully, you can use assertive communication. This means being honest while still respecting others' feelings. Active listening is a big part of this. It means really paying attention when others speak, nodding, or giving a quick answer, "I see" to show you're engaged. When it's your turn to talk, use assertive body language. Stand or sit up straight, look people in the eye, and speak with a steady voice. These small actions help convey confidence and ensure your message is heard. Practicing these skills regularly can make speaking up feel more natural over time.

Fear of judgment or rejection is common, but it doesn't have to hold you back. Building self-assurance takes practice. Start by speaking up in small ways, like answering a question in class or sharing a thought with a friend. Each time you do, it becomes easier. Positive visualization can also help. Before speaking, close your eyes and picture yourself expressing your thoughts clearly and being listened to. Imagine the calmness and confidence you feel in that moment. Visualization helps prepare your mind for success and reduces anxiety. Remember, everyone feels nervous sometimes, and that's okay. It's a part of growing and learning.

Advocacy and leadership are powerful ways to use your voice. They allow you to stand up for what you believe in and make a difference. Consider joining student councils or clubs. These groups offer platforms to speak up for yourself and others. They teach you how to work with different people and present ideas in a way that inspires action. Participating in public speaking events, like debates or presentations, can also boost your confidence. They provide opportunities to practice speaking in front of others, which helps you become more comfortable with your voice. Leadership isn't just about being in charge. It's about guiding others and making a positive impact.

Finding your voice is a journey of self-discovery. It's about understanding what you care about and sharing it with the world. Speaking up allows you to connect with others, bring about change, and grow as a person. It empowers you to influence your surroundings and inspire those around you. As you continue to explore this chapter, remember that your voice is a tool. It's there to express your brilliant ideas and share your unique perspective. Embrace it, nurture it, and watch as it opens doors to new possibilities and connections.

6

CELEBRATING DIVERSITY AND CULTURE

I magine sitting in a room filled with people from all around the world. Each person wears a unique outfit and shares stories from their culture. You hear different languages, taste new foods, and see dances you've never seen before. This is what makes our world so special. Each culture has its own way of celebrating life's big moments, including puberty and periods. These traditions offer a glimpse into how different people experience the same changes. Let's explore some of these amazing rites and what they mean.

Despite the diverse ways cultures celebrate puberty and first periods, there are universal experiences we all share. Hormonal changes and growth spurts are a part of growing up, no matter where you are. These changes can feel awkward and exciting all at once. Emotions might bounce around like a ping-pong ball, but that's okay. It's a normal part of becoming who you are. Across cultures, these changes mark new beginnings. They signal a time of learning and growth, where you start to understand yourself better. It's a time when you begin to see the world through new eyes.

Menstruation, too, is a universal experience, though cultures view and handle it differently. In some African communities, girls might spend time in menstrual huts. These huts offer a space for rest and reflection during menstruation. While this might seem unusual, it's a tradition that holds cultural significance. In Japan, the first period is often met with quiet acknowledgment. Some families might celebrate with a special meal or a small gift, marking the occasion with respect and understanding. These customs show that menstruation is a natural and important part of life, worthy of recognition and care.

The first period, or menarche, is a significant milestone in many cultures, often symbolizing a girl's transition to womanhood. Here's an overview of how various cultures have historically acknowledged this event and the rituals or traditions surrounding it:

6.1 CULTURAL TRADITIONS AROUND THE WORLD

1. **India**:
   o **Hindu Traditions**: In South India, especially among Tamil and Telugu communities, menarche is celebrated with a grand ceremony called *Ritu Kala Samskara* or *Sadangu*. The girl is treated as a bride for the day, given new clothes, and adorned with jewelry. The event is a community celebration symbolizing fertility and womanhood.
   o In some tribal communities, rituals include isolating the girl during her first period for a few days to symbolize her transition.

2. **Japan**:
   - In historical Japan, there weren't grand celebrations, but families might quietly acknowledge the milestone. Traditionally, a girl would be given a red piece of cloth as a symbolic gesture representing menstruation.
3. **Native American Cultures**:
   - Many Native American tribes have rich ceremonies for a girl's first period. The Apache tribe, for example, holds the *Sunrise Ceremony*, a four-day event that celebrates a girl's transformation into womanhood with dances, prayers, and blessings.
4. **Jewish Traditions**:
   - In Orthodox Jewish communities, menarche marks the beginning of teaching about *niddah*, the laws of family purity. While there isn't a ritual to celebrate menarche itself, it signifies readiness for deeper religious observances. In Jewish tradition, a Bat Mitzvah marks a special time for girls. At age 12, a girl celebrates her Bat Mitzvah, which means "daughter of the commandment." This ceremony signifies her commitment to her faith and her responsibilities within the Jewish community. It's a big celebration. Friends and family gather to honor this important milestone. The girl often reads from the Torah, showing she has learned about her religion and is ready to take on new roles. It's a time of pride and joy, celebrated with music, dancing, and delicious food.
5. **Latin America**:
   - In many Latin American cultures, a girl's first period may coincide with her *quinceañera* (15th birthday celebration), a larger rite of passage acknowledging her maturity. Menarche might also be marked with small

familial celebrations or gifts. A celebration of a girl's 15th birthday with a Quinceañera in Hispanic culture marks her transition to womanhood. It often starts with a religious ceremony, followed by a big party. The girl wears a beautiful dress, often in pastel colors, and her family and friends join in the festivities. A special dance with her father and a toast mark the occasion. The Quinceañera is not just a party. It's a meaningful event that honors family, tradition, and the journey to adulthood. It's a chance for the community to come together and show support for the young girl.

6. **African Traditions**:
   - Among some African tribes, menarche is celebrated with elaborate rites of passage. For instance, in Zambia's Bemba tribe, the *Chisungu* ceremony involves teaching the girl about womanhood, marriage, and societal expectations.

7. **Western Cultures**:
   - Historically, in Western cultures, menarche was often a private family matter with little celebration. However, in recent years, some families have embraced giving gifts or organizing small gatherings to make the experience positive and empowering for young girls.

8. **Islamic Cultures:**
   - A girl who starts menstruating becomes *mukallaf*, meaning she is now accountable for performing Islamic tradition, menarche is considered a significant moment because it marks a girl's entry into a stage of greater religious responsibility. While there isn't a specific ritual tied to menarche in Islamic teachings, its implications are deeply rooted in religious practice and cultural variations:

- Religious duties like daily prayers (*salah*), fasting during Ramadan and observing Islamic laws of modesty (*hijab* if applicable)
- Menstruating women are exempt from fasting and prayers during their periods and are encouraged to engage in other acts of worship, like *dua* (supplication) or reading Islamic literature.
- In many Islamic communities, families celebrate this milestone privately, sometimes by giving the girl gifts or organizing a small gathering to acknowledge her transition into womanhood.
- Emphasis is often placed on teaching about cleanliness (*taharah*) and menstrual hygiene, as this is a crucial part of Islamic practice.

9. **Pacific Island Cultures**:
   - In many Polynesian cultures, a girl's first period is seen as a reason for celebration. For example, in Samoa, this event might involve a family gathering to honor the girl's transition to adulthood.

6.2 THEMES ACROSS CULTURES

Despite differences, common themes in acknowledging menarche include:

- **Education**: Teaching the girl about her body and responsibilities.
- **Celebration**: Recognizing her transition into womanhood, often with gifts or ceremonies.
- **Community Support**: Providing emotional and cultural reinforcement of her new identity.

Learning about these cultural practices can broaden our understanding and appreciation of the world. Trying out traditional recipes from different cultures can be a fun way to experience their flavors and customs. You might find a new favorite dish or learn about the ingredients that hold cultural significance. Likewise, learning greetings or phrases in other languages can open doors to new friendships and connections. It shows respect and interest in other cultures, fostering an environment of inclusion and understanding. Embracing diversity enriches our lives and helps us see the beauty in our differences.

Interactive Activity: Cultural Exploration

- Choose a country or culture you're curious about.
- Research a traditional dish from that culture and try making it at home.
- Learn a few greetings or simple phrases in the language spoken there.
- Share your experience with friends or family and discuss what you learned.

Celebrating diversity means recognizing the shared experiences that unite us while honoring the unique traditions that make each culture special. By exploring these practices, we gain a deeper appreciation for the rich tapestry of humanity.

6.3 EMBRACING DIVERSITY: STORIES FROM GIRLS LIKE YOU

Imagine Priya, an Indian girl attending a multicultural school. She sits in class surrounded by friends from all over the world. Each lunchtime, they share different foods and stories. Priya loves these moments, but she also feels the weight of balancing her cultural traditions with the modern world she navigates daily. At home, her family speaks Hindi, celebrates Diwali with bright lights and sweets, and wears traditional clothes. At school, Priya switches to English, joins sports teams, and dresses in jeans and t-shirts. She sometimes feels torn between two worlds, unsure of where she fits in. Priya's story is about finding harmony between her rich heritage and the new experiences that shape her. She learns to blend the two, like a beautiful dance, finding strength in her unique identity.

Then there's Elara, a Native American girl who lives on a reservation. She feels deeply connected to her community and family. Every summer, her family gathers for a powwow, a celebration of dance, music, and tradition. Elara feels a strong sense of belonging here. She listens to stories from her elders, learning about her tribe's history and values. But when she leaves the reservation for school, Elara faces challenges. She encounters people who don't understand her culture. Some days, she feels like she's carrying the weight of her ancestors on her shoulders. Yet, Elara finds strength in her roots. Her family's stories empower her to educate others about her culture, breaking down barriers and building bridges of understanding.

These girls face unique challenges. Balancing cultural traditions with modern expectations is not easy. Priya worries about fitting in while honoring her family's ways. Elara strives to share her culture without losing herself in a world that doesn't always understand. Both girls show resilience, overcoming hurdles with determination. They learn to stand tall and embrace their backgrounds, turning challenges into triumphs. Priya's success in bridging two cultures inspires her peers. She starts a cultural club at school, where students celebrate their heritage through food, stories, and art. Elara's efforts to educate others lead to a cultural exchange program, where students visit her reservation to learn firsthand about her tribe.

Language can be a big hurdle, too. Priya remembers her first day at school, stumbling over words in English. She felt embarrassed, but her classmates' patience and kindness helped her learn. Now, Priya is fluent and confidently switches between languages. She even teaches her friends a few Hindi phrases, fostering a deeper connection. Elara, meanwhile, works to preserve her native language. She participates in language classes, ensuring the words of her ancestors continue to live on. These achievements are significant. They show how overcoming language barriers can open doors to new friendships and opportunities.

Sharing stories is powerful. They have the ability to connect us and build empathy. Imagine a classroom filled with students, each taking turns to share their tales. You hear about Priya's dual life and Elara's cultural pride. These stories create a tapestry of experiences, weaving together lessons of resilience and hope. They remind us that, despite our differences, we share common struggles and dreams. Writing prompts can help you reflect on your own stories. Think about what makes you unique, the challenges you've faced, and the victories you've achieved. Pen your thoughts in a journal or share them with friends. Ask your parents and grandparents for help in understanding your own family culture and how you can preserve your family roots and traditions. As women and mothers, someday, you will teach them to your children so your family culture and traditions will remain alive and taught to the next generations. These reflections can help you see the beauty in your journey.

Creating a storytelling event in your classroom or community can be a wonderful way to share and connect. Invite classmates to bring a story, a song, or an artifact from their culture. As you listen to each other, you'll discover new perspectives and build a stronger sense of community. You might find that someone else's story mirrors your own or teaches you something new. These events encourage dialogue and foster a spirit of inclusion, where everyone's voice is heard and valued.

Empathy and connection grow from relating to others' experiences. When you hear Priya's story, you might see a bit of yourself in her. Maybe you've felt out of place, too. Or perhaps Elara's journey resonates with you, reminding you of your own cultural pride. Discussing these similarities helps build bridges between hearts. Group activities, like cultural fairs or pen pal exchanges, can deepen these connections. They offer a chance to learn and grow together, celebrating both our shared humanity and the unique colors each of us brings to the world.

6.4 BODY IMAGE AND MEDIA: SEEING BEYOND THE SCREENS

Think about the last time you scrolled through social media. You probably saw pictures that seemed perfect. Maybe there was someone with flawless skin or another person with an amazing outfit. It might have made you feel like you needed to match up to this image of perfection. But here's a secret: a lot of what you see online isn't the full picture. Social media often uses filters and editing tools to create images that aren't real. These tools can smooth out skin, change body shapes, and add effects that don't exist in real life. They create an illusion that can make us feel like we need to look a certain way to be accepted. The truth is, these images are often far from reality. Understanding this can help you see beyond the screens.

Movies and TV shows also play a big role in shaping how we view beauty. They often cast people who fit a narrow standard of what's considered attractive. This can lead us to believe that only certain body types and appearances are beautiful. But beauty is diverse, and it comes in many forms. Recognizing this diversity helps us appreciate the unique qualities in ourselves and others. It's important to remember that what we see on screen is often scripted and doesn't reflect real life. Everyone has their own beauty, and it's not limited to what we see in the media.

When you look at these images, take a moment to compare them with real life. Think about the people around you—your family, friends, and classmates. Notice the differences and diversity in their appearances. Creating a collage of diverse beauty can be a fun way to celebrate this. Cut out pictures from magazines or print them from online sources. Include images of people of different ages, sizes, and backgrounds. This collage can serve as a reminder that beauty is not one size fits all. It's a powerful tool to help you reject harmful beauty standards and embrace your own unique beauty.

Being media savvy means questioning the things we see and hear. Start by identifying biases in advertising and marketing. Ads often show the best possible version of a product or an idealized lifestyle. They can make us feel like we need to buy something to be happy or accepted. But remember, ads are designed to sell, not to tell the whole truth. Discussing the power of influencers and celebrities can also be eye-opening. Many influencers use their platforms to promote products and lifestyles. It's important to remember that they get paid to do this. Not everything they show is genuine. By recognizing these tactics, you can become more critical of the media you consume and make choices that align with your values.

Celebrating your individuality is about embracing what makes you unique. Practicing daily affirmations can help build a positive self-image. Start each day by saying something kind to yourself, like "I am unique and valuable" or "My differences make me beautiful." These affirmations can help shift your focus from trying to fit in to a certain worldly mold set by advertisers to sell their products or programs and instead appreciating who you are. Engaging in activities that celebrate diverse beauty is another way to empower yourself. Consider participating in art projects that highlight this diversity. You might create a mural with friends that showcases different cultures and experiences. Or, organize a photo project that celebrates natural beauty in your community. These activities can help you see the beauty in diversity and encourage others to do the same.

It's not always easy to look beyond the images we see every day. But by questioning what we see by celebrating the reality of those images, "Are they real? Am I believing a lie from advertisers or from a magazine or website selling products?" By celebrating our uniqueness, we can start to change how we view beauty. Embrace diversity, and remember that everyone's beauty is special in its own way. A very pretty person can be very ugly because of their self-centeredness, as can an ordinary person be so beautiful because they love and care for others, and that is beauty that somebody cannot fake. Outward appearance is only skin deep; look into the heart and see if it's genuine.

6.5 CELEBRATING DIFFERENCES: EVERY BODY IS UNIQUE

Imagine standing in a room full of people, each one different in size, shape, and color. Some are tall, some are short. Others might have curly hair, freckles, or dimples. Each person is like a piece of art, unique and beautiful in their own way. These differences make our world vibrant and interesting. It's important to embrace what makes us different. Your height, weight, and features are all a part of who you are. They tell your story. Instead of wishing to change them, celebrate them. They're part of what makes you, you. When you look in the mirror, try to see the beauty in your own reflection. Notice the little things that make you stand out, and remember that they are your signature, your unique mark on the world.

But beauty isn't just about what we see. It's also about what we do and how we feel. Your abilities and talents are just as important as how you look. Maybe you're great at singing or have a knack for solving math problems. Perhaps you have a special way of making people laugh. These skills and qualities are part of what makes you special. They define you in ways that go beyond appearance. Focus on these strengths. They have the power to build your confidence and make you feel proud of who you are. Recognizing what you're good at can open doors to new opportunities and friendships. It can help you connect with others who share your interests and passions.

Body image challenges are something many people face, especially women and girls. It's easy to fall into the trap of negative self-talk, telling yourself you're not good enough. But you can fight back against these thoughts. Start with positive affirmations. Each morning, stand in front of the mirror and say something kind to yourself. It might feel strange at first, but over time, these words can change how you see yourself. They help replace doubt with confidence. Engaging in body-positive activities can also help. Dance, pilates or yoga are great choices. They allow you to move your body in ways that feel good. They remind you of your strength and grace. These activities focus on what your body can do, rather than how it looks.

Imagine a world where everyone practices acceptance and kindness. It starts with small acts. Be kind to yourself. Treat yourself with the same care you would show a friend. Think about the negative self-talk you say or think about yourself; you would never say it to someone's face, especially out loud. Be kind to yourself, be thankful. You are fearfully and wonderfully created to be just who you are; celebrate your unique self. When you speak to yourself, use gentle words. This kindness can extend to others, too. Celebrate the differences you see around you. When you notice someone's unique style or talent, give them a compliment. These small gestures create a ripple effect, spreading positivity and acceptance. They help build a community where everyone feels valued and included. Group discussions and projects are another way to celebrate differences. They offer a chance to learn from each other and share experiences. These conversations can lead to greater understanding and empathy.

Think about the last time you did something kind for someone. Maybe you helped a friend with homework or gave a stranger a smile. These acts of kindness make a big difference. They create connections and lift others up. They remind us that we're all in this together. By practicing acceptance and kindness, you contribute to a more inclusive and loving world. You help create a space where everyone feels free to be themselves, without fear of judgment. This culture of acceptance starts with you. It grows each time you choose to see the beauty in yourself and others. It thrives when you embrace differences and celebrate the unique qualities that make each person special.

6.6 THE POWER OF WORDS AND EMOTIONS

Picture this: you're in the schoolyard, chatting with friends. The sun is warm on your face, and laughter fills the air. Then, someone makes a comment. It's just a few words, but they sting. Maybe it was meant as a joke, or maybe not. Yet, those words linger, affecting how you feel for the rest of the day. That's the power words hold. They can lift you up, but they can also tear you down. Being careful with your words is important. Think of them as tiny seeds. Once spoken, they can grow into something beautiful or something that hurts. Don't let hurtful words from others take root; seek to find good instead; if the words have some truth in them and it's something you can change for the better, use it to grow yourself for the better; if it's not, don't let it stick to you. Choosing kind and supportive words can make a big difference. Positive words can brighten someone's day, just like a ray of sunshine.

Now, think about the words you say to yourself. We all have an inner voice, like a friend who's always with us. Sometimes, that voice can be kind, saying things like, "You did a great job" or "You're amazing just the way you are." Other times, it might not be so nice, saying things like, "You'll never get it right" or "Why can't you be like them?" It's easy to be hard on ourselves, but it's just as important to be uplifting. Treat yourself like you would your best friend. Would you tell them they aren't good enough? Probably not. So why say it to yourself? Being kind to yourself can boost your confidence and help you feel more positive.

Being kind to others is just as important. Think about how it feels when someone is kind to you. Maybe they help you with homework or say something nice about your new outfit. It feels good, doesn't it? That's the magic of kindness. It's like a gentle ripple that spreads, touching everyone it meets. Treating others how you would like to be treated is the simple golden rule that can have a big impact. It's about empathy. It's about understanding that everyone has their struggles, even if they don't show it. A kind word or a small gesture can make someone feel seen and valued.

Imagine a world where words are used to encourage, not to hurt. It starts with you. You have the power to choose your words and use them wisely. It's about being mindful of what you say and how it might affect others. Before speaking, take a moment to think. Ask yourself if what you're about to say is true, helpful, and kind. If it isn't, consider finding a better way to express yourself. This doesn't mean you can't be honest. It means being honest with care and respect.

Remember honesty is best if it will help someone, not to destroy them. We all do enough destructive self-talk of our own. Be the positive friend, give good feedback, be the friend they need.

Emotions are closely tied to the words we use. They can color our interactions, influencing how we react to situations. When you're feeling upset or angry, it's easy to let words slip out that you might not mean. But taking a moment to pause can help. Take a deep breath. Think about how you feel and why. This can help you respond more thoughtfully rather than reacting in the heat of the moment. It's a skill that takes practice, but it's worth it. It can help you communicate better and strengthen your relationships. It's the best way to be a true friend, and you will attract trustworthy and kind friends. It's a win-win situation!

Think of your words as tools. They can build bridges or create walls. They can heal or hurt. By choosing to be careful with your words, you create a space where understanding and compassion can grow. You learn to listen, not just to others, but to yourself. You become aware of how your words can affect the world around you. This awareness is powerful. It can lead to a more positive and loving environment where everyone feels respected and valued. It's essential that you learn these lessons and skills so that when you are a mother or mentor of the next generation, you can lead the way to a better world that lifts others up and makes a difference for the good of everyone.

As you continue your journey, remember the power of your words. Use them to uplift, to connect, and to spread kindness. You have the ability to make a difference, one word at a time. Let your words reflect the kindness and empathy you wish to see in the world. This chapter closes with an invitation to carry these lessons forward. As you explore the next chapter, think about how you can continue to use your voice for good. Let your words be a beacon of light, guiding others and yourself toward a brighter, more kinder world in the future.

7

OVERCOMING CHALLENGES

I magine sitting in class when the teacher asks you to speak in front of everyone. Your heart races and your cheeks turn red. You feel all eyes on you like the spotlight is too bright. This is a common moment of embarrassment many people face. Embarrassment can feel like a wave crashing over you, leaving you unsure of what to do next. It happens to everyone; it's especially stressful during puberty when so many changes are happening. Understanding why we feel embarrassed can help us handle it better. It might be a simple mistake, like stumbling over words during a presentation. Or it might be more personal, like realizing you have a mustard stain on your clothes from your messy lunch today. These moments are part of life. They help us grow and learn to laugh at ourselves.

Public speaking often tops the list of embarrassing scenarios. Standing in front of a room full of peers can feel intimidating. It's like everyone is waiting for you to mess up. But remember, it's not about being perfect. It's about sharing your ideas. Everyone makes mistakes, even adults. When you speak, focus on your message. Imagine you're talking to a friend. Take a deep breath before you start. This helps calm your nerves and gives you a moment to gather your thoughts. You can also prepare a mental script. Think about what you want to say and practice it a few times. This way, you'll feel more confident when it's your turn to speak.

Experiencing period leaks or stains can also cause embarrassment. You're sitting in class, and suddenly, you realize there's a period stain on your pants. It feels like the end of the world, but it's not. Every woman has been in the same situation at one time or another. Carrying an extra pair of clothes in your bag can help you feel prepared. If it happens, excuse yourself to the restroom and take care of it. If you are caught unprepared, no worries, you can ask to go to the school nurse. Remember, these things happen to everyone. They're just part of life. Staying calm and taking action will help you handle the situation with grace.

Exercise: Build Your Calm Kit

- Choose a few small items that help you feel calm and confident.
- It might be a favorite pen, a smooth stone, or a small notebook for doodling.
- Strong mints, chocolate, gum, or sour sweets.
- Fidget spinners, silly putty, digital journal, or stress ball.
- Keep these items in your bag to use when you feel embarrassed or stressed.

Try this informal trick for dealing with anxiety: The 333 Rule: Look around to identify 3 objects and 3 sounds, then move 3 body parts. Many people find this strategy helps them focus and stay grounded when their anxiety seems overwhelming. You can do it without anyone knowing, and it can keep you in the game.

Finding humor in awkward moments can make them less daunting. Imagine you trip in the hallway and drop your books. Instead of feeling embarrassed, you laugh and say, "Well, that's one way to make an entrance!" Sharing these funny stories with friends can also help. It turns an awkward moment into a shared laugh. Humor is a powerful tool. It lightens the mood and reminds us that it's okay to be imperfect. When you're kind to yourself, it's easier to move past embarrassment. Self-compassion means treating yourself like you would a good friend. If a friend tripped, you'd probably laugh it off with them and help them up. Do the same for yourself, like Arianna did.

Arianna sat in her seat, chewing the end of her pencil as she tried to solve the next math problem. Her focus was interrupted by a strange, warm sensation. At first, she brushed it off, thinking it might just be nerves. But as the minutes ticked by, the feeling didn't go away. Finally, curiosity got the best of her. She glanced down and froze—there was a small red stain on the chair.

Her heart began to race. Could this be her first period? It wasn't supposed to happen yet! Arianna didn't have any supplies, and she had no idea what to do. What if someone saw? The thought of her classmates laughing or pointing made her stomach twist.

She considered staying silent and hoping the stain wouldn't get any worse, but deep down, she knew she needed help. Gathering every ounce of courage, Arianna raised her hand.

"Yes, Arianna?" her teacher asked.

Arianna leaned forward and whispered, "Can I go to the nurse's office? It's... kind of urgent."

The teacher nodded with understanding and handed her a hall pass without asking any questions. Arianna quickly tied her jacket around her waist and hurried to the nurse's office, her cheeks burning the whole way.

When she arrived, the nurse greeted her warmly. "Hi, Arianna. What's going on?"

Arianna hesitated for a moment before blurting out, "I think I started my period, and I don't have anything with me."

The nurse smiled kindly. "That's no problem at all. It happens to everyone." She handed Arianna a pad and showed her how to use it, then offered her an extra pair of gym shorts to change into. "You're all set. And don't worry, if you ever need anything, you can always come here."

Arianna felt a wave of relief wash over her. She changed and returned to class, feeling a lot calmer. No one noticed she had been gone, and the day continued without any drama. By the time she got home, she was proud of herself for speaking up and handling her first period like a pro.

Building resilience through these experiences is key. Each time you face embarrassment and bounce back, you get stronger. Reflect on past experiences. Think about a time you felt embarrassed. How did you handle it? What did you learn? Celebrate the small victories. Maybe you spoke in front of the class and didn't faint. Maybe you handled a stain quietly and confidently. These moments show you that you can handle embarrassment. They prove that you're resilient and capable. Getting through them builds confidence over time. Remember, everyone experiences these moments. They are opportunities to grow and learn. Embrace them, laugh them off, and keep moving forward.

7.1 MANAGING PERIODS IN PUBLIC: CONFIDENCE ON THE GO

Imagine you're out shopping with friends or at a school event, and suddenly, you realize your period has started. It can feel like a mini panic attack, but it doesn't have to be. Being prepared is key to managing periods confidently when away from home. Start by putting together a discreet period kit. This can be a small pouch with a few pads, tampons, or a menstrual cup, along with some wet wipes and an extra pair of underwear. Keep this kit in your backpack, locker, or purse so you're always ready. Knowing you have what you need can ease your mind and help you focus on enjoying your day. Planning bathroom breaks is also a smart move. Pay attention to your body's signals and try to time your bathroom visits as needed. That way, you have a moment to check in and make sure everything is good.

When it comes to managing your period discreetly, a little creativity goes a long way. Choose period products that come in quiet packaging. This way, you can grab what you need without drawing attention. Consider wearing dark or patterned clothing, which can help hide any potential leaks. Comfort is important, too. Opt for clothes that make you feel good and allow you to move freely. This might mean choosing stretchy leggings or a flowy dress. These small choices can boost your confidence and help you feel more at ease.

Preparation and planning are your best friends. Keep spare supplies in multiple locations. Maybe stash a few items in your locker, backpack, and even at a friend's house. This way, you're covered no matter where you are. Use the reminder feature on your phone to prompt you to change your period products. It's easy to lose track of time when you're busy, so a little nudge can be helpful. These simple actions take just minutes to set up but can save you from stressful situations later.

Don't be afraid to ask for help if you need it. If you find yourself without supplies, reach out to a friend or teacher. Most people understand and are willing to help. Your school nurse can be a great resource, too. If you're at a public place, like a mall or restaurant, remember that many women have been in your shoes. They know what it's like and are often willing to lend a hand or spare pad if you ask. It can feel awkward at first, but remember, asking for help shows strength, not weakness. There's a kind of sisterhood when it comes to periods. We all know what it's like, and there's comfort in that shared understanding.

7.2 DEALING WITH UNPREDICTABLE CYCLES: WHAT TO DO

Your menstrual cycle can sometimes feel like it's playing a game of hide and seek. One month, it's on time, and the next, it's nowhere to be found. And that's perfectly normal, especially during puberty. Your body is still figuring things out, and this can lead to irregular cycles. Hormones are like little messengers in your body. They tell your ovaries when to release an egg and your uterus when to prepare for it. When these hormone levels shift, it can make your cycle unpredictable. Stress and lifestyle changes can also throw things off. If you're worried about a big test or going through changes at home, it might affect your period. Even things like travel or a new exercise routine can have an impact. Life can be unpredictable, and sometimes your period follows suit.

To get a better handle on your cycle, tracking it can be really helpful. There are many apps for tracking your cycle, like Clue or Flo. They let you record when your period starts and ends and even track symptoms like cramps or mood changes. This information helps you spot patterns over time. Maybe you notice that your period tends to be late after a stressful week. Or you realize that you always feel more tired a few days before it starts. Recognizing these patterns, like breast tenderness, backaches, acne breakouts, etc., can help you feel more in control. It's like having a map that leads you through unfamiliar territory. Plus, when you visit a doctor, having this information handy can make it easier to discuss any concerns.

Despite your best efforts, sometimes your period will surprise you. That's why having your emergency period kit can save the day. Keeping a small bag with pads, tampons, or a menstrual cup, some wipes, and spare underwear in your bag so you're always prepared, no matter where you are. This way, if your period starts unexpectedly, you have everything you need to handle it. Knowing you're prepared can reduce anxiety and help you feel more confident.

Keeping a health journal can also be a great tool. Try writing down any physical symptoms you notice, like cramps or headaches. Also, note any emotional changes, like feeling extra sensitive or irritable. Over time, you might see connections between your symptoms and your cycle. Maybe you notice that certain foods make cramps worse or that you feel better when you exercise. Sharing this journal with a healthcare provider can give them valuable insights. It helps them see the bigger picture and offer advice tailored to your needs. It's also a way to remind yourself that you're in tune with your body.

These unpredictable cycles can be a bit tricky, but it's all part of the process. It's about learning to work with your body and understanding its unique rhythms. With a little preparation and awareness, you can navigate these challenges. Remember, you're growing up and changing, and so is your body. It's all part of becoming your fantastic self.

7.3 WHEN TO SEEK HELP: UNDERSTANDING MEDICAL CONCERNS

Puberty comes with its ups and downs, and sometimes it might feel like your body is throwing a party you didn't plan. While most changes are normal, some things might need a little extra attention. If you ever find yourself doubled over with cramps that just won't quit or your period is so heavy that you're changing pads or tampons more often than usual, it's time to pause and think about seeking help. Severe cramps can sometimes signal that your body needs a bit more care. Heavy bleeding might mean it's time to talk to someone who knows about these things. Skin issues, like acne that just won't clear up, can also be frustrating. While some pimples are expected, persistent, painful acne might need a doctor's advice. Knowing when to seek help is part of taking care of yourself.

Now, how do you know when it's time to call in the pros? If symptoms stick around longer than what seems normal or they start interfering with your day-to-day life, it's worth talking to a doctor. Maybe those cramps keep you from joining your friends for a weekend hangout. Or perhaps your skin feels so painful that you avoid certain activities. These are signs that professional help could make a difference. Remember, doctors are there to help, not judge. They have seen it all and are ready to give you the support you need. Think of them as team players in your journey to feeling your best.

When you're ready to chat with a healthcare provider, it helps to be prepared. Write down any questions you have before the appointment. Maybe you're wondering if your symptoms are normal or if there's a treatment that could help. List these questions so you don't forget them when you're face-to-face with the doctor. Describe your symptoms clearly. Instead of saying, "I don't feel well," try to be specific. Mention when the symptoms started, how often they occur, and what makes them better or worse. This helps the doctor understand what you're going through and how best to help.

Talking to a trusted adult about your health is an important step. It might feel a bit awkward at first, but remember, they care about you and want to help. Share your concerns with a parent, guardian, or another adult you trust. They can offer advice, help you decide if it's time to see a doctor, and even come with you to appointments. Having someone there can make the experience feel less scary. If you're not comfortable discussing certain topics, it's okay to ask for a female doctor or nurse. Your comfort and safety are important, and healthcare providers understand this. It's your body, and you have the right to feel safe and respected.

Being open about your health concerns is part of growing up. It's all about learning to listen to your body and knowing when to ask for help. You're not alone in this. Many girls and every woman have been where you are, and there's a whole community ready to support you. It's okay to reach out and say, "Hey, I could use some help here." That's not a sign of weakness. It's a sign of strength and self-awareness.

7.4 ADDRESSING BODY IMAGE ISSUES: BUILDING SELF-ESTEEM

Growing up means facing all kinds of changes, and sometimes it feels like everyone has an opinion about how you should look. From glossy magazine covers to endless social media feeds, as women, we are bombarded with images of what's considered beautiful. Reminding ourselves that we are fearfully and wonderfully created to be just as we are can not be stated enough. It truly is a woman's battle with self-esteem issues and self-doubt. These images often show perfect bodies, flawless skin, and never a hair out of place. It's easy to start comparing yourself to these pictures and wonder why you don't look the same. But here's the thing: those images aren't real life. They're often edited and staged to look a certain way, and they don't show the true diversity of beauty. Besides media, there's also pressure from peers. You might feel like you need to fit in by looking or dressing a certain way. But everyone is unique, and that's what makes you special.

Building a positive body image starts with changing how you see yourself. Practicing positive affirmations can help.

Stand in front of the mirror and say something kind about yourself.

Focus on your inner qualities. Maybe you're a great friend, a talented artist, or really good at making people laugh.

Remind yourself of these strengths every day. It might feel strange at first, but over time, these words will become part of how you see yourself. Engaging in activities that highlight your personal strengths is another way to boost self-esteem. If you love sports, join a team. Enjoy writing? Start a journal or blog. These activities help you focus on what you're good at rather than what you look like.

Puberty brings a lot of changes that are unfamiliar and seem odd. Don't get hung up on today; you are a beautiful butterfly in its early transformation stage, changing into a soon full-grown spectacular woman before long.

Self-care is also crucial in building self-esteem. Self-care days are a wonderful way to nurture yourself. Spend a day doing things you love, whether it's reading a book, taking a walk, or watching your favorite movie. These moments remind you to be kind to yourself and appreciate who you are. Self-compassion is about treating yourself with the same kindness and understanding you'd show a friend. If your friend made a mistake, you wouldn't be harsh with them, so don't be harsh with yourself.

Celebrating diverse body types is important, too. Embrace the diversity in appearance and abilities. Look for role models who reflect a variety of body images. Maybe it's a musician who rocks their unique style or an athlete who inspires you with their strength. Seeing diverse role models reminds you that beauty comes in all shapes and sizes. It's a powerful reminder that you're not alone in this journey. You're part of a community that values you just as you are. Be the best you you can be! Remember, self-esteem isn't about fitting into someone else's mold. It's about embracing who you are and celebrating your unique qualities.

7.5 HANDLING EMOTIONAL OVERWHELM: TOOLS FOR BALANCE

Puberty can feel like you're on a roller coaster with no brakes. One minute, everything seems manageable; the next minute, it all feels like too much. Emotions run high, and it's normal to feel overwhelmed. School demands play a huge part. Assignments pile up, and teachers and parents expect you to do your best. It feels like you're juggling a dozen balls, trying not to drop any. Social changes add another layer. Friends might change, and relationships shift. Navigating these dynamics can feel like solving a complex puzzle. You're learning about yourself, and that's a big deal. These changes can easily lead to feeling emotionally overloaded.

Finding ways to manage these feelings is important. Mindfulness meditation is a great tool. It helps calm your mind and brings you back to the present.

Take a few minutes each day to sit quietly. Focus on your breathing. Let your thoughts come and go without holding onto them. This practice can help you feel centered and less stressed. Prayer can also offer comfort if it's something you practice. It allows you to reflect and find peace.

Setting realistic goals is another key. Break tasks into smaller steps. This makes them more manageable and less intimidating.

Prioritize what needs to be done first. It's okay to focus on one thing at a time.

Talking to someone you trust can make a big difference. Friends and family are there to listen.

Sharing your feelings can lighten the load. They might offer advice or simply be there for support. Sometimes, just knowing someone cares helps. Often, saying out loud what's going on in your life helps you see it more clearly, and you can see solutions by sharing it with others you trust. If you're finding it hard to cope, joining a support group or talking to a counselor can be beneficial. These spaces offer a chance to connect with others who understand. You'll find you're not alone. Many people feel the same way. They can share tips and experiences that help you see things in a new light.

Keeping balance in your life is crucial for emotional health. Engage in activities you enjoy. Hobbies provide a break from stress and let you express yourself. Whether it's painting, dancing, or playing an instrument, find something that brings you joy. Regular physical activity also helps. Exercise releases endorphins, the body's natural mood boosters. Even a short walk can help clear your mind. Don't forget the importance of rest. Adequate sleep is essential. It recharges your body and mind, making it easier to handle challenges. Create a bedtime routine that helps you unwind. Turn off screens and relax before sleep. This helps you get the rest you need.

Maintaining balance isn't just about managing stress. It's about nurturing your well-being. When you feel balanced, it's easier to face challenges. You're more resilient and better equipped to handle whatever comes your way. Life has its ups and downs. That's okay. It's about finding what works for you and using those tools to keep yourself steady. You're growing and learning, and that's something to be proud of. Finding balance helps you enjoy the present and look forward to the future. As you continue to navigate these changes, remember you're not alone.

You have the strength and support to thrive.

As we close this chapter, hold onto the idea that balance is key. Emotions are part of life's ebb and flow, and you're learning to ride the waves. Up next, let's explore how to embrace new beginnings with curiosity and courage.

8

EMPOWERMENT AND GROWTH

Have you ever watched a butterfly emerge from a cocoon? At first, it struggles, its wings crumpled and wet. But as it stretches, those wings unfold into a beautiful masterpiece, ready to take flight. Puberty can feel a bit like this transformation. It's a time when you face many changes, both inside and out. These changes might seem overwhelming, but they are part of your growth. Just like that butterfly, you're getting ready to spread your wings. This chapter is about embracing these changes with confidence. It's about understanding that each step is a chance to discover more about who you are.

During puberty, your body and mind are in a constant state of change. It's like you're on a journey to meet new parts of yourself. These changes aren't just physical. They involve your emotions, thoughts, and how you see the world. Viewing these changes as opportunities can help you grow in ways you never imagined. You might find that you're more sensitive to the feelings of others or that you have new interests. These shifts are signs that you're developing in a healthy way. Puberty is a time for self-improvement and discovery. It's a chance to explore who you are and who you want to become.

Adaptability is an important part of this growth. Being open to new experiences can help you learn more about yourself. Trying a new hobby or activity can be a great way to explore your interests. Maybe you've always wanted to try ceramics or join a robotics team. Now is a perfect time to give it a go. You might discover talents you didn't know you had. Along the way, you'll face challenges and make mistakes. But that's okay. Mistakes are just steps on the path to learning and growing. They teach you valuable lessons and help you become stronger.

Self-reflection is a powerful tool for personal growth. It's like a mirror that shows you where you've been and where you're going. Keeping a personal growth journal can help you track your progress. Write about your experiences and what you learn from them. Set aside time each week to reflect on your thoughts and feelings. This practice can help you understand yourself better and make sense of your emotions. It's like having a conversation with yourself, where you can explore your dreams and goals. Over time, you'll see how much you've grown and changed.

As you grow, you'll notice that your identity is evolving. This is a natural part of becoming who you are meant to be. Embrace these changes and celebrate your uniqueness. Explore new interests and passions. Maybe you'll find a love for music or a knack for science. Whatever it is, let it be a part of your evolving identity. Celebrate your milestones and progress, no matter how small they may seem. Each step forward is a victory. Remember, you're not the same person you were yesterday. You're constantly growing and changing, and that's something to be proud of.

Puberty is a time of transformation, much like the butterfly's journey. Embrace each change and challenge with confidence, knowing that they are shaping you into the person you are meant to become.

8.1 SETTING GOALS: PLANNING FOR YOUR FUTURE

Have you ever thought about what you want to achieve? Setting goals is like creating a map for your future. It helps you find direction and gives you the motivation to reach your dreams. Imagine you're on a road trip. You need a destination and a route to get there. Goals are like the stops along the way that guide you. They help you stay focused and keep you moving forward. Setting goals also breaks down big dreams into small steps. This makes them easier to handle. You can see your progress as you achieve each small goal, and this keeps you motivated to continue.

There are different types of goals you can set. Some are short-term, like weekly or monthly goals. These are great for improving skills or completing small projects. Maybe you want to read a book by the end of the month or learn a new song on the piano. Short-term goals give you quick wins and build your confidence. Then, long-term goals take more time, like academic achievements or personal dreams. These might include getting good grades or learning a new language. Long-term goals require patience and planning, but they can be very rewarding. Both types are important because they keep you moving toward what you want in life.

Setting realistic goals takes practice, but it's worth the effort. One helpful method is the SMART framework. SMART stands for Specific, Measurable, Achievable, Relevant, and Time-bound. Let's say you want to improve your math skills. A SMART goal would be, "I will practice math problems for 30 minutes, five days a week, for the next month to improve my test scores." This goal is specific and measurable, with a clear timeline. It's also achievable and relevant to your growth. Another fun way to set goals is to create a vision board or goal chart. Use pictures, words, and drawings to represent your goals. Hang it where you can see it every day. It will remind you of what you're working toward and keep you inspired.

SMART Goals

S   Specific

What am I going to do? Why is this important to me?

M   Measurable

How will I measure my success? How will I know when I have achieved my goal?

A   Attainable

What will I do to achieve this goal? How will I accomplish this goal?

R   Relevant

Is this goal worthwhile? How will achieving it help me? Does this goal fit my values?

T   Time-Bound

When will I accomplish my goal? How long will I give myself?

Regularly checking your goals is important. Just like you wouldn't drive without checking your map, you shouldn't set goals without reviewing them. Take time to see how you're doing.

S	Specific What am I going to do? Why is this important to me?
M	Measurable How will I measure my success? How will I know when I have achieved my goal?
A	Attainable What will I do to achieve this goal? How will I accomplish this goal?
R	Relevant Is this goal worthwhile? How will achieving it help me? Does this goal fit my values?
T	Time-Bound When will I accomplish my goal? How long will I give myself?

Celebrate your successes, no matter how small. If something isn't working, adjust your goals.

Maybe you discover a new interest or realize a goal needs more time. It's okay to change your goals to match your interests and values. This flexibility helps you stay true to yourself. It also keeps you motivated and focused on what matters most to you.

Setting goals is a powerful way to plan for your future. It helps you take control of your life and make your dreams a reality. With clear goals and a plan, you can achieve anything you set your mind to.

8.2 ROLE MODELS: LEARNING FROM OTHERS' JOURNEYS

Think about someone you admire. Maybe it's a teacher, a family member, or even a character from a book. Role models play a big part in how we see the world and ourselves. They can inspire you to try new things and show you what's possible. Through their stories, you learn about overcoming obstacles and finding success. Role models teach you about perseverance. They show you that even the toughest challenges can be faced with courage. When you see someone's achievements, they can light a fire inside you. They make you believe you can do it, too. They offer different perspectives, helping you see things from new angles.

Good role models have certain qualities that make them stand out. Integrity is one of them. It means doing the right thing, even when no one is watching. It's about being honest and true to yourself. Authenticity is another. Being genuine means being real, showing your true self without pretending. Role models who are passionate about what they do inspire others. They show dedication to their craft or cause, working hard to make a difference. These qualities make them people worth looking up to. You can learn a lot by watching how they handle life's ups and downs.

It's important to seek role models from different backgrounds. Diversity enriches your understanding of the world. Explore individuals from various cultures and industries. You might find role models in unexpected places. They could be artists, scientists, athletes, or activists. Each one brings unique experiences and insights. Reading biographies is a great way to learn about their lives. You get a glimpse into their struggles and triumphs. Documentaries can also be inspiring, showing real-life stories and allowing you to connect with their journeys.

Don't forget to look close to home, too. Ask your mom, sister, aunt, or grandmother about their experiences. They all have stories to tell, especially about their own puberty and period journeys. Listen to how they coped with challenges. You might be surprised by what you learn. Their stories might show you how things have changed over time. Or maybe how some things remain the same. These personal connections are valuable. They provide wisdom and understanding, helping you navigate your own path.

These times let you hear directly from the people you admire. You can ask questions and gain insights that aren't found in books. Reflect on the lessons they share and think about how their stories relate to your experiences. What can you learn from their successes and failures? How can you apply their wisdom to your own challenges? This reflection helps you grow. It turns inspiration into action, guiding you as you move forward.

Role models have the power to shape who you are. They influence your dreams and aspirations. By learning from their stories, you gain courage and confidence to pursue your own goals. You discover that you can overcome obstacles, just like they did. You find the strength to keep going, even when things get tough. Role models remind you that you are capable of greatness, no matter what you face.

8.3 YOUR SUPPORT NETWORK: BUILDING A CIRCLE OF TRUST

Picture this: you're having a rough day. Maybe school was tough, or you're just feeling down. In times like these, having a circle of people who support you can be a lifesaver. These people are your support network. They offer you emotional support and encouragement. They listen when you need to talk and give advice when you're unsure. Surrounding yourself with people who lift you up can make all the difference. They help you feel understood and less alone, especially during challenging times. Think of them as your personal cheerleaders, always ready to help you find your way.

So, who makes up this important network? Start with family members and close friends. These are people who know you well and care about your well-being. They are the ones you can call when you need a shoulder to lean on. Mentors, teachers, or coaches also can play a key role. They offer guidance and wisdom from their own experiences. Maybe there's a teacher who always has a word of encouragement or a coach who believes in your potential. All these people contribute to a strong support system. They each bring something unique that helps you feel secure and supported, like Jazzmon with her grandma Ruby..

Jazzmon sat cross-legged on her bed, her phone resting in her lap. She stared at the screen, biting her lip. She had so many questions swirling in her mind, but she wasn't sure how to start. Her mom was working late, and her best friend, Lila, didn't have her period yet. There was one person Jazzmon trusted to tell her the truth without making her feel silly—Grandma Ruby.

Taking a deep breath, Jazzmon dialed her grandmother's number. It only rang twice before the warm, familiar voice picked up.

"Hi, sweet pea! What's going on?" Grandma Ruby asked.

"Hi, Grandma," Jazzmon said, her voice trembling slightly. "I... I need to talk to you about something kinda personal."

"Of course, honey. You can tell me anything."

Jazzmon hesitated for a moment before blurting it out. "I think I'm about to get my period, but I don't know what to do. My body's changing, and it's just... weird."

"Oh, sweet girl," Grandma Ruby said gently, "I remember feeling the same way when I was your age. You're not alone, and there's nothing to be scared of. Your body's just growing up, and that's a beautiful thing."

Jazzmon exhaled, her shoulders relaxing a little. "But what if it happens at school? What if I get a stain on my pants? Everyone will laugh at me!"

Grandma Ruby chuckled softly. "Let me tell you a little trick: You just wrap a jacket around your waist and keep your head high. Most people are too busy worrying about their own stuff to notice. Remember you have your period kit ready in your backpack."

Jazzmon smiled, feeling a flicker of confidence. "That's actually really smart, Grandma. Thanks."

"Anytime, sweetheart. And remember, I'm always here if you have more questions. This is just the start of a big, beautiful adventure of becoming a young woman."

Jazzmon felt a warmth spread through her chest. "I love you, Grandma."

"I love you too, Jazzmon. Now go grab some chocolate—it's the best medicine for just about everything!"

Jazzmon laughed, her nerves melting away. She didn't have all the answers yet, but with Grandma Ruby by her side, she knew she'd be okay.

Keeping these relationships strong takes effort. Open and honest communication is key. Share your thoughts and feelings with those you trust. Let them know what's going on in your life. This openness builds trust and deepens your connections. It's important to show appreciation and gratitude regularly. A simple thank you or a kind gesture can mean a lot. It shows that you value the relationship and care about the person. These small acts keep your bonds healthy and strong. It reminds them that they matter to you.

Sometimes, you need to expand your support network. Meeting new people can bring fresh perspectives and new friendships. Joining clubs or youth groups is a great way to do this. Find a club at school that matches your interests or a faith-based youth group that aligns with your passions. Volunteering opportunities and serving others is another excellent way to meet like-minded individuals. Helping others not only feels good, but it also connects you with people who share your values. These new connections can become a valuable part of your support network.

Your support network is like a garden. It needs care and attention to grow. With the right people around you, you'll find it easier to face challenges and celebrate successes. They'll be there to cheer you on and offer a helping hand when you need it. So, take the time to nurture these relationships and seek out new ones. They are an important part of your life, offering love, support, encouragement, and guidance every step of the way.

8.4 SELF-DISCOVERY: EMBRACING YOUR UNIQUE PATH

Have you ever thought about what makes you, you? Puberty is a time when you start to look inward. You begin to explore who you are and what matters to you. It's like opening a book where each page reveals something new about yourself. During this time, you'll notice your strengths and weaknesses more clearly. You might find that you're a great listener or that you love solving puzzles. Understanding these aspects helps you identify your passions. Are you drawn to music, art, or science? Finding what excites you gives you clues about your identity. These interests are part of what makes you unique.

Exploration is key during this phase. Trying new things helps you learn more about yourself. You might take up a new hobby or join an extracurricular activity. Maybe you've always been curious about painting or coding. Now is the perfect time to give it a try. You'll never know what you're capable of until you explore. Don't be afraid to step out of your comfort zone. Exploring different career paths or academic subjects can also be eye-opening. Attend a club meeting or a cooking class. You might discover a new interest that leads you in an exciting direction. This experimentation is all about finding what fits you best.

Sometimes, it's hard to figure out where to start. That's where tools for self-discovery come in. Personality assessments can help you learn more about your traits. They might show you that you're creative or analytical. Interest inventories can guide you toward activities you might enjoy.

Reflective journaling is another great tool. Writing about your day and what you enjoyed helps you uncover patterns in your likes and dislikes. It's like having a conversation with yourself.

These exercises provide insights that can guide your decisions and help you understand yourself better.

Being true to yourself is crucial. Embrace your true self without worrying about what others think. Practicing self-acceptance and self-love are important steps. It's about being okay with who you are, even if you're different from others. Everyone is unique, and that's something to celebrate. Your individuality is your strength. Don't be afraid to stand out. Celebrate your quirks and what makes you special. This authenticity is your superpower. It helps you connect with others who appreciate you for who you are. When you accept yourself, you open the door to a world where you can be your best self.

It's easy to get caught up in what others expect from you. But remember, this is your path. No one else can walk it for you. Trust in your instincts and follow what feels right. Surround yourself with people who support your journey of self-discovery. They can offer encouragement and remind you of your worth. As you explore your identity, you'll find new layers to who you are becoming, growing into an amazing young woman. Each discovery is a step toward becoming the person you want to be. Embrace this time of exploration and growth. It's a chance to learn, to change, and to celebrate the amazing woman you are becoming.

EMPOWERMENT AND GROWTH | 139

8.5 CELEBRATING YOU: ACKNCWLEDGING YOUR ACHIEVEMENTS

Think back to a time when you accomplished something big or small. Maybe it was acing a test you studied hard for, or perhaps it was learning a new skill, like riding a bike without training wheels. How did that make you feel? Celebrating your achievements, no matter their size, is super important. It's like giving yourself a high five and saying, "I did it!" Recognizing your successes boosts your self-esteem and gives you a push to aim even higher next time. It reminds you of your ability to overcome challenges and grow. Reflecting on these moments helps you see how far you've come. It's a way to look back and say, "Wow, I really did that."

Sharing your accomplishments with people who support you can make the celebration even sweeter. Tell your family or friends about your successes. They are there to cheer you on. Their excitement and pride add to your own joy. It's like you're all celebrating together, and that makes the moment even more special. When you share your wins, you inspire others, too. They see what you've achieved and think, "If they can do it, maybe I can too." Your success becomes a light that guides others, showing them what's possible when you put your mind to it.

Keeping track of your achievements is a great way to stay motivated. Try maintaining an accomplishment journal. Write down your successes, big and small. Include how you felt and what it took to get there. Over time, you'll build a collection of rewards, medals, trophies, and ribbons that highlight your growth. You can also create a visual achievement board. Fill it with pictures, drawings, or graded papers that represent your accomplishments. Hang it where you can see it every day. This visual reminder keeps you focused on your goals and encourages you to keep going. It's like having a personal cheerleader reminding you of your victories and potential.

Celebrating your achievements doesn't have to be elaborate. Sometimes, a small celebration is the most meaningful. Plan a little treat for yourself, like a special dessert or a fun outing. Share your success with a mentor or role model. Their feedback and support can boost your confidence and give you that extra encouragement to keep pursuing your dreams. Celebrations are about acknowledging your hard work and dedication. They're a way to say, "I deserve this moment."

Gratitude plays a big role in celebrating your achievements. It's important to thank those who supported you along the way. Maybe it's a friend who helped you study or a teacher who gave you guidance. Expressing gratitude strengthens your relationships and shows that you appreciate their help. Reflect on the journey that led to your success. Think about the lessons you learned and the obstacles you overcame. These reflections help you grow and prepare for future challenges. They remind you that every step, even the tough ones, was worth it.

As you move forward, remember to celebrate each achievement. Whether it's a small victory or a major milestone, take the time to acknowledge your hard work. These moments of celebration fuel your passion and motivate you to keep reaching for new heights. They remind you of your strength and resilience. So, let each success be a stepping stone to the next, guiding you on your path to greatness.

CONCLUSION

As you reach the end of this book, I hope you feel more equipped to handle the changes that come with puberty. We've journeyed together through many topics. We've talked about how your body changes. We've learned about growth spurts, menstruation, and the different ways your body might surprise you. Understanding these changes is important. It helps you feel less alone and more prepared.

We also explored the emotional shifts that happen during this time. Puberty can feel like an emotional roller coaster. But remember, these feelings are normal. Building emotional resilience is key. It helps you manage those ups and downs with confidence. Self-care is another important part of growing up. Taking care of your body and mind should be a priority. From hygiene to nutrition, each small habit contributes to your overall well-being.

Navigating social interactions can be tricky. Friendships may change, and peer pressure might try to steer you in different directions. But with the right tools, you can handle these experiences. Embrace your individuality. Celebrate the beauty of who you are becoming, a woman, possibly a wife someday and even a mother. You are a one of a kind, special, unique, fearfully and wonderfully created person. It's these differences that make us special.

Throughout these chapters, we've touched on empowerment and growth. Embracing your body and your emotions. How to build strong relationships and cherish your individuality. These are the lessons I hope you carry forward. You have the strength within you to face any challenge.

Remember, puberty is just one part of your lifelong journey. It's a time of discovery. But it doesn't end here. Keep exploring your interests. Find what makes you happy and brings you joy on the inside. Set goals and work towards them. The world is full of possibilities waiting for you.

I want to encourage you to apply what you've learned in this essential girl's guide to growing up strong, to growing into a well rounded and capable woman. Practice the self-care routines we discussed. Use the communication strategies to express yourself clearly. Try the confidence-building exercises. Share your stories with friends. Support one another. You are not alone. Together, you can create a supportive community.

As your guide, I am so grateful you chose this book. Thank you for letting me be a part of your growing-up journey. I'm here to remind you that you can do this. You are strong. You are capable. And you are never alone.

As you move forward, remember that you are amazing just as you are. Embrace your unique path with pride. You have the power to shape your future. Trust in yourself. You are resilient. And the possibilities ahead of you are endless.

Keep shining bright, and never stop believing in yourself. Your journey is just beginning, and I can't wait to see all the incredible things you will do.

You've got this!

THANK YOU FOR READING!
NOW, LET'S HELP OTHERS TOGETHER

You've made it through *The Essential Girl's Guide to Puberty & Periods*—congratulations! Armed with the knowledge and confidence from this guide, you're ready to navigate puberty like a pro.

Now, you have the chance to pay it forward.

By leaving an honest **review on Amazon**, you're not just sharing your thoughts—you're helping other girls, parents, teachers, and even grandparents discover this guide. Your feedback could be the reason someone else gains the tools to handle their puberty journey with confidence and courage.

YOUR VOICE MATTERS

When you share your experience, you're making a real difference. Your insights might help another young woman overcome her fears, embrace changes, and feel more prepared for this important stage of life.

IT ONLY TAKES A MOMENT

Scan the QR code to leave your review and
share how this book made a difference for
you or your family:

THANK YOU FOR BEING PART OF THIS JOURNEY

Your support helps keep this essential guide alive and available for
those who need it most. I can't thank you enough for your kindness
and generosity in sharing your thoughts.

Together, we're making puberty a little less scary and a lot more
manageable—for everyone.

With heartfelt gratitude,

DebbieAnn

REFERENCES

What is a Growth Spurt During Puberty? https://www.hopkinsmedicine.org/health/ wellness-and-prevention/what-is-a-growth-spurt-during-puberty

Tanner Staging https://www.mtnstopshiv.org/sites/default/files/attach ments/TannerStaging2.pdf

What Can I Do About Acne? (for Teens) https://kidshealth.org/en/teens/prevent-acne.html

Puberty - Hormonal Changes - Physical Changes https://teachmephysiology.com/ reproductive-system/development-maturation/puberty/

Understanding the Four Phases of the Menstrual Cycle https://www.morelandobgyn. com/blog/4-phases-of-the-menstrual-cycle

Best Period Tracker Apps Reviewed: Manage Your Teen's Cycle https://www.knix teen.com/blogs/the-rag/the-best-teen-and-tween-period-apps

Eco-Friendly Options for Menstrual Products https://www.webmd.com/women/ features/eco-friendly-options-for-menstrual-products

8 Period Myths We Need to Set Straight https://www.healthline.com/health/womens-health/period-myths

Effects of Teenage Hormones On Adolescent Emotions https://www.newportacad emy.com/resources/empowering-teens/teenage-hormones-and-sexuality/

Stress Management and Teens https://www. aacap.org/AACAP/Families_and_Youth/Facts_for_Families/FFF-Guide/Helping-Teenagers-With-Stress-066.aspx

Teaching Body Positivity to Young Girls - CeCe Olisa https://ceceolisa.com/teaching-body-positivity-to-young-girls/

24 Positive Self-Talk Activities for Kids and Teens https://veryspecialtales.com/posi tive-self-talk-kids/

Hygiene Basics (for Teens) | Nemours KidsHealth https://kidshealth.org/en/teens/ hygiene-basics.html

Nutrition in the adolescent - PubMed https://pubmed.ncbi.nlm.nih.gov/10036686/

Importance of Sleep for Teenagers https://qatar-weill.cornell.edu/institute-for-popula tion-health/community/stay-safe-stay-healthy/issue/importance-of-sleep-for-teenagers

75 Mindfulness Activities for Teens, Worksheets, & Questions https://www.carepa tron.com/guides/mindfulness-activities-for-teens

Friendship: Just The Facts https://www.healthforteens.co.uk/relationships/friend ships/friendship-just-the-facts/

Chapter 4: Social Media and Romantic Relationships https://www.pewresearch.org/ internet/2015/10/01/social-media-and-romantic-relationships/

Helping Kids Deal With Bullies (for Parents) https://kidshealth.org/en/parents/ bullies.html

Assertiveness (for Teens) | Nemours KidsHealth https://kidshealth.org/en/teens/ assertive.html

13 Amazing Coming of Age Traditions From Around the ... https://www.globalciti zen.org/en/content/13-amazing-coming-of-age-traditions-from-around-th/

Menstruation and Cultural Practices: Diverse Traditions ... https://www.pinkishe. org/blog-post/menstruation-and-cultural-practices-diverse-traditions-around-the-world

Social Media's Effect on Self-Esteem: How Does It Affect ... https://socialmediavic tims.org/mental-health/self-esteem/

20 Positive Body Image Activities & Worksheets for Teens ... https://veryspecialtales. com/positive-body-image-activities-and-worksheets-teens/

Helping Kids Deal with Embarrassment https://childmind.org/article/help-kids-deal-embarrassment/

Getting your period at school: 5 tips for stress-free periods https://helloclue.com/arti cles/cycle-a-z/getting-your-period-at-school-5-tips-for-stress-free-periods

Irregular Periods (for Teens) | Nemours KidsHealth https://kidshealth.org/en/teens/ irregular-periods.html

Body Image and Self-Esteem (for Teens) | Nemours KidsHealth https://kidshealth. org/en/teens/body-image.html

The Development of Self and Identity in Adolescence https://pmc.ncbi.nlm.nih.gov/ articles/PMC6667174/

How to Help Teens Set Effective Goals (Tips \u0026 Templates) https://biglifejournal. com/blogs/blog/guide-effective-goal-setting-teens-template-worksheet?srsltid= AfmBOoo68eT_IVq9taB8eg_1i4gCkxwUiZ-7HJeEJNl2KsJ9PbwsrTrb

10 Women Role Models + Ideas for Sparking Kids' Passions https://lingokids.com/ blog/posts/10-inspiring-female-role-models-for-children

Building Support Networks for Teen Mental Health https://hopenationcounseling. com/resources/support-networks-for-teen#

GLOSSARY OF TERMS

Puberty can feel overwhelming with so many new things to learn, but don't worry—you're not alone! This glossary explains important words you'll see in the book. If you're unsure about a term, come back to this page anytime to find its meaning.

A

Acne: Small bumps or pimples that can appear on your skin, especially your face, during puberty because of hormonal changes.

Adolescence: The stage between being a child and an adult when your body and mind are growing and changing.

B

Balance: Learning to manage school, friendships, family, and self-care in a healthy way.

Blemishes: Small marks, spots, or imperfections on the skin, often caused by clogged pores, excess oil, or bacteria. They are common during puberty due to hormonal changes.

Blood: The red fluid that carries oxygen and nutrients in your body. During your period, blood is released from the uterus as part of menstruation.

Breasts: The part of a girl's body that develops during puberty and plays a role in breastfeeding later in life.

C

Clitoris: A small, sensitive part of the vulva that plays an important role in how the body feels. It is located near the top of the vulva.

Cramps: A tightening feeling in your lower belly during your period, caused by your uterus shedding its lining.

Crush: A strong feeling of admiration or affection, often for someone you find interesting, attractive, or fun to be around. For middle schoolers, a crush is usually an innocent and exciting feeling that might make you want to spend more time with or think about that person a lot.

Confidence: Believing in yourself and your abilities, even when facing challenges or changes.

Cultural: Customs, traditions, and practices that vary by region, family, or group, including those related to puberty and periods.

Cycle: The process of your period that repeats every month, usually lasting about 28 days.

D

Diet: The food you eat every day, which can affect how you feel during puberty and your period. Eating balanced meals helps your body stay healthy.

Discharge: A clear or white fluid that comes from your vagina as part of your body's way of staying clean and healthy.

E

Emotions: Feelings like happiness, sadness, anger, or excitement, which can be stronger during puberty because of changing hormones.

Egg: Also called an ovum, it is the female reproductive cell stored in the ovaries. Each month, during ovulation, one egg is released from an ovary and travels through the fallopian tube. If the egg is not fertilized by a sperm cell, it breaks down and is shed along with the uterine lining during menstruation. Girls (females) are born with all the eggs they will ever have, and the number decreases over time.

Estrogen: A hormone in your body that helps with growth, periods, and other changes during puberty.

F

Fallopian Tubes: The tubes in your body that connect your ovaries to your uterus.

Fatigue: Feeling very tired, which can happen before or during your period.

G

Glands: Small parts of your body that release hormones to help with growth and other changes.

Growing-Up: The process of maturing physically, emotionally, and mentally as you transition from a child to a young adult.

H

Hormones: Chemicals in your body that act as messengers, helping your body grow and change during puberty.

Hygiene: Keeping yourself clean and healthy, especially during your period.

I

Imbalance: When your hormones or emotions feel "off," which is normal during puberty.

L

Labia: The soft folds of skin around the opening of the vagina.

Lining (Menstrual Lining): The tissue inside your uterus that thickens every month and is shed during your period as menstrual fluid.

M

Menarche: The first occurrence of menstruation in a female, marking the onset of puberty and the beginning of reproductive capability. This natural biological milestone typically occurs between the ages of 9 and 16 and is influenced by factors such as genetics, health, and environment.

Menstrual Cup: A small, reusable cup made of silicone or rubber that you insert into your vagina to collect period blood.

Menstrual Fluid: The mix of blood and tissue that comes out of your body during your period.

Menstruation (Period): When your body releases blood and tissue from the uterus as part of your monthly cycle.

Mood Swings: Quick changes in how you feel. like going from happy to sad, caused by hormones.

N

Natural: Approaching puberty and self-care in a way that feels comfortable and true to yourself.

O

Ovaries: Two small organs in your body that release eggs and hormones like estrogen and progesterone.

Ovulation: When your ovary releases an egg as part of your monthly cycle.

P

Pads:(Sanitary Pads) A soft, absorbent product worn inside underwear to absorb menstrual blood during a period. Sanitary pads come in various sizes and thicknesses to suit different flow levels and personal preferences. They often have an adhesive strip on the bottom to keep them securely in place and may include wings that fold over the sides of underwear for added protection against leaks. Pads are disposable and should be changed regularly to maintain hygiene and prevent odors.

PMS (Premenstrual Syndrome): The physical and emotional symptoms you may feel before your period, like cramps, tiredness, or mood changes.

Period Panties: Special underwear designed to absorb period blood and keep you feeling dry and comfortable, that provides built-in protection against menstrual leaks. Period panties are made with absorbent and leak-proof layers to catch menstrual blood, and they can be worn alone or as backup with other menstrual products like pads, tampons, or cups. They come in various styles and absorbency levels, offering a comfortable, reusable, and eco-friendly option for managing periods. Period panties are machine washable.

Pregnancy: The period when a fertilized egg grows and develops into a baby inside the uterus. It typically lasts about nine months.

Puberty: The time when your body begins to change from a child to an adult.

R

Romance: A special emotional connection or feeling of affection between two people, often involving admiration, kindness, and a desire to spend time together. For middle schoolers, it might mean having a crush or enjoying the company of someone who makes you feel happy and valued.

S

Sanitary Products: Items like pads, tampons, menstrual cups, or period panties used during your period.

Self-Care: Taking care of your body, mind, and feelings, especially during big changes like puberty and periods.

Shaving: Removing hair from your legs, underarms, or other areas, which some people choose to do for personal or cultural reasons.

Sperm: Male reproductive cells that are essential for fertilization. They are produced in the testes and can join with a female's egg to create a pregnancy.

T

Tampons: Small, soft tubes you can use during your period to absorb blood from inside your body.

Testosterone: A hormone everyone has, but boys usually have more of it.

U

Uterine Lining: The layer of tissue inside the uterus that thickens each month in preparation for a possible pregnancy. If pregnancy does not occur, the lining is shed during menstruation.

Uterus: The part of your body where a baby can grow one day. During your period, the uterus sheds its lining.

V

Vagina: The part of your body that connects the outside of your body to your uterus.

Vulva: The outside part of your private area, including your labia and clitoris.

Waxing: A method of hair removal where warm wax is applied and then pulled off, removing hair from the root.

W

Wellness: Feeling healthy and balanced in your body and mind.

Z

Zits: Another word for pimples or spots that may appear during puberty.

www.ingramcontent.com/pod-product-compliance
Lightning Source LLC
Chambersburg PA
CBHW071153120626
46546CB00006B/2250

* 9 7 8 1 9 6 8 2 0 8 0 1 1 *